Assignmen
Punctuation and
Spelling
for reinforcement and revision

Eric Williams

Edward Arnold

First published 1977
by Edward Arnold (Publishers) Ltd
41 Bedford Square, London WC1B 3DQ

Reprinted 1978, 1979, 1982

ISBN: 0 7131 0101 6

Acknowledgments

The Publisher's thanks are due to the following for permission to reproduce copyright material in this book:

London Express News and Feature Services for an extract from Delia Smith's *Evening Standard Cookery Book*; Penguin Books Ltd for an excerpt from Peter Terson's *Zigger Zagger* (Penguin Modern Playwrights 1970), pp. 50–51 © Peter Terson 1970; Associated Newspapers Group Ltd for two Fred Bassett strip cartoons which originally appeared in the London *Daily Mail*.

Printed and bound in Great Britain at
The Camelot Press Ltd, Southampton

Contents

3 Spelling—introductory

4 Spelling—sounds

Preface

This book is intended for use by students in F.E. Colleges and Schools preparing for external examinations. It can be used by students working individually or for group discussion, and can be worked through as a revision course, or, by referring to the Contents and (in respect of the spelling assignments) the Checklist, the teacher can set individual assignments as an aid to correcting mistakes in spelling and punctuation. The assignments draw the student's attention to patterns in spelling and punctuation and have been compiled following a survey of errors made by candidates for G.C.E. Ordinary Level English Language examinations.

All definitions, phonetic spellings and etymologies are taken from *Chambers's Students' Dictionary*.

1 Punctuation—full stop, comma, colon, semi-colon

1.1.1   *Separate the six sentences in this passage with full stops. Each time you begin a new sentence, start with a capital letter.*

once there were three men travelling in an aeroplane unfortunately, one fell out fortunately, there was a haystack below him unfortunately, there was a pitchfork in the haystack fortunately, he missed the pitchfork unfortunately, he missed the haystack

Add stops and capital letters to the following passage:

a magician had a pet parrot that was part of his show the parrot had seen the tricks so many times that he was very bored then the magician got a job entertaining the passengers on an ocean liner he pulled rabbits out of a hat and then made them disappear he waved his hands and made a pack of cards vanish into thin air all the time the parrot sat on his perch and sourly watched the same old show suddenly the boilers in the engine room exploded during a performance and the ship sank there was nothing left on the ocean but the magician and the parrot sitting at opposite ends of a big plank curiosity finally overcame the parrot grudgingly he said, 'All right, I'll buy it what did you do with it'

1.1.2   Note the differences in these sentences:

Gorillas live in tropical forests, where they climb trees in search of food.

Gorillas live in tropical forests, and they climb trees in search of food.

Gorillas, which live in tropical forests, climb trees in search of food.

Gorillas live in tropical forests, climbing trees in search of food.

Gorillas live in tropical forests. They climb trees in search of food.

A comma is used to show a pause inside a sentence, separating one part from another to avoid confusion.

For instance, an introductory word or phrase needs to be marked off with a comma:

By the way, gorillas live in tropical forests.

Incidentally, gorillas climb trees in search of food.

Each of the following sentences needs a comma to mark off an introductory word or phrase. *Read each sentence aloud to decide where the comma should be placed:*

By the way I saw Mike last night.

Funnily enough he was carrying a picnic hamper again.

As you know the last time we saw him he was trying to get one onto a bus.

However this time it wasn't his uncle's.

Nevertheless it still looked too heavy for him.

Indeed he was sweating and grunting as if he were training for weight-lifting.

On the other hand it may just be that he's still feeling weak after our trek.

Similarly, there may be an additional piece of information at the end of the sentence which will be marked off by a comma, as has happened here. This information, on the other hand, may come in the middle. If so, separate it with a pair of commas.

However, this time it wasn't his uncle's.

This time it wasn't his uncle's, however.

This time, however, it wasn't his uncle's.

Add single commas or pairs of commas to the following sentences, as appropriate:

Now and again through the black mass of drifting cloud came a straggling ray of moonlight which lit up the expanse.

It appeared to me that amongst so many old foundations there might be still standing a house in which though in ruins I could find some sort of shelter for a while.

Indeed I found a low wall encircling the copse.

Presently I found an opening with a square mass of some kind of building beyond.

Just as I caught sight of this however the drifting clouds obscured the moon.

I passed up the path in darkness shivering.

I groped my way blindly on hoping for shelter.

Somewhere ahead I hoped would be a log fire as well as food and a warm drink.

Each of these sentences contains a phrase that needs to be marked off with commas. The phrase gives additional information about the first word in the sentence.

Italian, a beautiful language, is fairly easy to learn.

Rome, the capital of Italy, is a beautiful city.

If the phrase were removed, the sentence would still make sense:

Italian is fairly easy to learn.
Rome is a beautiful city.

The pair of commas is being used like a pair of brackets:
Rome (the capital of Italy) is a beautiful city.

Rome, the capital of Italy, is a beautiful city.

In this example, the phrase 'the capital of Italy' could be used instead of 'Rome' to start the sentence:
The capital of Italy is a beautiful city.

Thus the single word 'Rome' could be inserted in the same way:
The capital of Italy, Rome, is a beautiful city.

Look carefully at the following sentences, noting where commas are added. Can you explain why?
Florence is a city in northern Italy.

Florence contains many art treasures.

A city in northern Italy contains many art treasures.

Florence, a city in northern Italy, contains many art treasures.

A city in northern Italy, Florence, contains many art treasures.

The technical term, by the way, for a word or passage of comment or explanation inserted in a sentence that is grammatically complete without it is *parenthesis*. An example of parenthesis is the phrase 'by the way' in the last sentence, where a comment is made.

Similarly, to remove the additional piece of information in parenthesis ('a city in northern Italy') in the sentence about Florence would still leave a complete sentence. A sentence might have a single word, a phrase, or a clause in parenthesis:

Mike, however, is strong for his age.

Mike, strong for his age, carried the picnic hamper by himself.

Mike, who is strong for his age, carried the picnic hamper by himself.

Mark off the words or passages of comment or explanation that are in parenthesis in the following sentences by using pairs of commas:

A sudden rather uncanny stillness made me stop.

The storm had passed and perhaps in sympathy with Nature's silence my heart seemed to cease to beat.

Suddenly the moonlight like a white finger pointed through the clouds.

A massive tomb of marble the square object before me was as white as the snow that lay around it.

Then while the flood of moonlight still fell on the marble tomb the storm resumed its course.

The graveyard a desolate scene seemed to shudder and groan.

I approached the tomb impelled by some sort of fascination to see what it was.

I walked around it and read graven in great Russian letters 'The Dead Travel Fast'.

On the top of the tomb seemingly driven through the solid marble was a great iron spike or stake.

I began to wish for the first time that night that I had taken Johann's advice.

With a terrible shock and under almost mysterious circumstances a thought struck me.

This was Walpurgis night when according to the belief of millions of people the devil was abroad.

On this night I suddenly realized the graves were opened and the dead walked freely.

This the very place the driver had specially shunned was the depopulated village of centuries ago.

A tornado of hailstones forced me to seek refuge in the only place available the deep Doric doorway of the marble tomb where I shivered and waited.

1.1.3 *Add commas, where appropriate, to the following passage:*
As I leaned against the door it moved slightly and opened inwards. The shelter of even a tomb was welcome in that pitiless tempest and I was about to enter it when there came a flash of forked lightning that lit up the whole expanse of heavens. In the instant as I am a living man I saw as my eyes were turned into the darkness of the tomb a beautiful woman with rounded cheeks and red lips seemingly sleeping on the bier. As the thunder broke overhead I was grasped as by the hand of a giant and hurled out into the storm. The whole thing was so sudden that before I could realize the shock moral as well as physical I found the hailstones beating me down. At the same time I had a strange dominating feeling that I was not alone. I looked towards the tomb. Just then there came another blinding flash which seemed to strike the iron stake that surmounted the tomb and to pour through to the earth blasting and crumbling the marble as in a burst of flame. The dead woman rose for a moment of agony while she was lapped in the flame and her bitter scream of pain was drowned in the thundercrash. The last thing I heard was this mingling of dreadful sound as again I was seized in the giant grasp and dragged away while the hailstones beat on me and the air around seemed reverberant with the howling of wolves. The last sight that I remembered was a vague white moving mass as if all the graves around me had sent out their sheeted dead and that they were closing in on me through the white cloudiness of the driving hail.

Here is the punctuation of the third sentence. Compare the writer's punctuation with your own, discussing why he has added commas where he has:
In the instant, as I am a living man, I saw, as my eyes were turned into the darkness of the tomb, a beautiful woman, with rounded cheeks and red lips, seemingly sleeping on the bier.

The clause 'as I am a living man' is in parenthesis, as is the phrase 'with rounded cheeks and red lips' (if the comma after 'lips' were left out, the result would be rather confusing!). Another example is in the sentence beginning 'The whole thing . . . '. Where?
The whole thing was so sudden that, before I could realize the shock, moral as well as physical, I found the hailstones beating me down.

You may not have thought a comma necessary between 'that' and 'before' in this sentence, and in the following sentence you may have omitted a comma before the relative pronoun 'which':

> Just then there came another blinding flash, which seemed to strike the iron stake that surmounted the tomb and to pour through to the earth, blasting and crumbling the marble, as in a burst of flame.

Why are commas necessary before 'blasting' and 'as' in this sentence?

Try reading the sentence through aloud without making a pause before 'which'. A pause is natural here in a sentence of this length. It is a good practice to check your own writing as if reading it aloud. As you read through your work, checking your punctuation carefully, without necessarily reading it aloud (especially during an examination!), try to imagine the pauses you would make if you were speaking. You will find you make far fewer punctuation mistakes by checking in this way.

> *Read these sentences aloud, listening for the effect of the pauses made by the commas:*
>
> The last thing I heard was this mingling of dreadful sound, as again I was seized in the giant grasp and dragged away, while the hailstones beat on me, and the air around seemed reverberant with the howling of wolves.
>
> The last sight that I remembered was a vague, white, moving mass, as if all the graves around me had sent out their sheeted dead, and that they were closing in on me through the white cloudiness of the driving hail.

Notice how the writer stresses each adjective in the phrase 'vague, white, moving mass' by using commas to separate them. He does the same in an earlier sentence in the passage:

> At the same time I had a strange, dominating feeling that I was not alone.

The other commas in these sentences are being used for a different purpose: in each case they come before a word that is used to link groups of words that would otherwise be separate sentences—and thus need full stops to divide them. Here are the separate sentences:

> The last thing I heard was this mingling of dreadful sound. Again I was seized in the giant grasp and dragged away. The hailstones beat on me. The air around seemed reverberant with the howling of wolves.
>
> The last sight that I remembered was a vague, white, moving

mass. It was as if all the graves around me had sent out their sheeted dead. It was as if they were closing in on me through the white cloudiness of the driving hail.

The author has decided to combine each of these groups of sentences into one, showing the connection between them by using a link word (the term for this is *conjunction*) preceded by a comma:
The last thing . . . of dreadful sound, **as** again . . . dragged away, **while** . . . on me, **and** the air . . .

The last sight . . . moving mass, **as if** all the graves . . . dead, **and that** they . . .

How does the writer combine these pairs of sentences in the passage you have punctuated? Check that you have added the commas correctly:
The shelter of even a tomb was welcome in that pitiless tempest. I was about to enter it when there came a flash of forked lightning that lit up the whole expanse of heavens.

The thunder broke overhead. I was grasped as by the hand of a giant and hurled out into the storm.

1.1.4 Gorillas live in tropical forests, where/and they climb trees in search for food.
Gorillas live in tropical forests. They climb trees in search for food.

In the above examples, a comma is sufficient to separate the two statements about gorillas only when a linking word ('where'/'and') is used also to combine the two statements into one sentence (see 1.1.3 above). Commas are correctly used when you wish to show pauses *inside* sentences, not between them. Thus in the second example above, the two statements are separated by a full stop: a comma would be incorrect, as there is no link made between the two sentences.
The commas in this passage have been retained, but the full stops are missing. Add the missing full stops and capital letters (the number of sentences in each paragraph is given in brackets):
he found no sign of anything unusual he bathed in a cool, deep pool he revelled in the lonely little paradise lonely it certainly was, but the loneliness was part of its charm the stillness, the peace, the isolation of this beautiful backwoods lake delighted him the silence was divine he was entirely satisfied (7)

after a brew of tea, he strolled toward evening along the shore,

7

looking for the first sign of a rising fish a faint ripple on the water with the lengthening shadows made good conditions *plop* followed *plop*, as the big fellows rose, snatched at their food, and vanished into the depths he hurried back ten minutes later he had taken his rods and was gliding cautiously in the canoe through the quiet water (5)

so good was the sport, indeed, and so quickly did the big trout pile up in the bottom of the canoe, that despite the growing lateness, he found it hard to tear himself away 'one more,' he said, 'and then I really will go' he landed that 'one more', and was in the act of taking off the hook, when the deep silence of the evening was curiously disturbed he became abruptly aware that someone watched him a pair of eyes, it seemed, were fixed upon him from some point in the surrounding shadows (5)

the feeling stole over him without the slightest warning he was not alone the slippery big trout dropped from his fingers he sat motionless, and stared about him (4)

nothing stirred the ripple on the lake had died away there was no wind the forest lay a single purple mass of shadow the yellow sky, fast fading, threw reflections that troubled the eye and made distances uncertain there was no sound, no movement he saw no figure anywhere however, he knew that someone watched him, and a wave of quite unreasoning terror gripped him the nose of the canoe was against the bank in a moment, and instinctively, he shoved off and paddled into deeper water (9)

the water dripped slowly from his paddle, now lying across the thwarts there was no other sound the canvas of his tent gleamed dimly a star or two were out he waited nothing happened (6)

Now read the following passage aloud, then add the missing commas:
It was an awkward moment and he did not quite like it. He sat there with his back to the blazing logs a very visible object in the light while all about him the darkness of the forest lay like an impenetrable wall. He could not see a yard beyond the small circle of his camp-fire; the silence about him was like the silence of the dead. No leaf rustled no wave lapped; he himself sat motionless as a log.

Then again he became suddenly aware that the person who watched him had returned and that same intent and concentrated gaze as before was fixed upon him where he lay. There was no warning; he heard no stealthy tread or snapping of dry twigs yet the owner of those steady eyes was very close to him probably not a dozen feet away. This sense of proximity was overwhelming.

It is unquestionable that a shiver ran down his spine. This time moreover he felt positive that the man crouched just beyond the firelight the distance he himself could see being nicely calculated and straight in front of him. For some minutes he sat without stirring a single muscle yet with each muscle ready and alert straining his eyes in vain to pierce the darkness but only succeeding in dazzling his sight with the reflected light. Then as he shifted his position slowly cautiously to obtain another angle of vision his heart gave two big thumps against his ribs and the hair seemed to rise on his scalp with the sense of cold that gave him goose-flesh. In the darkness facing him he saw two small and greenish circles that were certainly a pair of eyes yet not the eyes of Indian hunter or of any human being. It was a pair of animal eyes that stared so fixedly at him out of the night.

(From 'Running Wolf' in *Tales of the Uncanny and Supernatural* by Algernon Blackwood)

1.1.5   *In the following passages a caret (⅃) marks where a full stop or comma is needed. Add the correct punctuation marks, and capital letters where needed.*

When the famous American ⅃ Daniel Webster ⅃ was a boy ⅃ he often went to school with dirty hands and face ⅃ the teacher finally warned him that she would cane him if he did not wash before class the next day ⅃ Daniel paid no attention ⅃ the next morning ⅃ the teacher told him to hold out a hand for inspection ⅃ he spat on his hand ⅃ rubbed some of the dirt on to his trousers ⅃ then showed it palm up ⅃ the teacher looked and shook her head ⅃ "Daniel ⅃ if you can find another hand in the room that's dirtier than this one ⅃ I'll let you off without caning" ⅃ Daniel immediately showed her his other hand ⅃

A television producer heard music in the street in front of his house one day ⅃ he looked out and saw an old man ⅃ a dog ⅃ and a horse ⅃ The dog was playing an accordion ⅃ and the horse sang ⅃ while the old man collected pennies from passers-by ⅃ The TV man was so impressed that he got the musicians a job at a thousand pounds a week in his show ⅃ but when the day of performance came they did not appear at the studio ⅃ later ⅃ the TV man found them again ⅃ still playing for street-corner audiences ⅃

"What's the matter with you?" the TV man asked the old

fellow who collected the pennies ⌃ "you could be making a thousand pounds a week   "

"No ⌃ my conscience hurt me ⌃" the old man answered ⌃ "I don't think it's fair to fool the television public ⌃ the truth is ⌃ that horse can't sing ⌃ the dog's a ventriloquist ⌃"

Little Priscilla's mother thought she was beginning to show off too much ⌃ one night ⌃ when guests came for dinner ⌃ Mother said ⌃ "If Priscilla comes in and tries to attract your attention ⌃ don't pay any attention to her ⌃ she's supposed to go to bed and stay there ⌃" Before long ⌃ Priscilla came downstairs ⌃ with nothing on but her underwear ⌃ she did not say a word as she tiptoed several times round the table ⌃ the guests did as they had been told ⌃ they pretended not to see her ⌃ after a while Priscilla went off to bed ⌃ looking surprisingly pleased with herself ⌃ next morning ⌃ Mother heard her say to her brother ⌃"I rubbed it on and it works ⌃ they didn't see me ⌃"

"Rubbed what on?"

"Mother's vanishing cream ⌃"

An old lady reported some time ago that two valuable rings of hers had been stolen ⌃ the rings were insured ⌃ and the insurance company sent her a cheque for £500 ⌃ shortly afterwards ⌃ the old lady found the rings ⌃ she had just forgotten where she had put them ⌃ then she wrote a letter to the insurance company:

"Since I wanted to do the right thing ⌃ I decided I couldn't keep both the rings and the money ⌃ I am sure you will be happy to know I have given the £500 to the Lord Mayor's Fund ⌃"

1.1.6   Note the positions of the commas when separating 'he said', 'she asked', etc., from what is actually spoken:

"No, my conscience hurt me," the old man answered.

Mother heard her say to her brother, "I rubbed it on and it works."

Add full stops and commas to the following passage, together with capital letters where necessary:

The vicar took one Monday morning off and went down to the club to play golf he met Sam Green there and they set off together to play a game the vicar was quite good at golf but Sam Green wasn't and he was having a very bad day he just couldn't get the ball into the hole every time he had to make a putt he missed saying, "Damn. Missed."

The vicar was getting a bit upset by this at last he said "I say Green do you mind not swearing" at the very next hole Green aimed from only two feet away and the ball went past "Damn. Missed" he said

The vicar was really put out this time: "Look here Green if you swear again God will hear you and strike you dead with lightning" Green tried very hard at the next hole he spent ages looking at the ball and moving leaves away from the grass and practising shots finally he hit the ball very gently and it stopped just two inches from the hole "Damn. Missed" cried Sam Green the heavens opened there was a tremendous crack of thunder a flash of lightning shot down from the sky and hit the vicar then a deep voice came from on high "Damn. Missed"

When interrupting a sentence that is spoken by 'he said', etc., a pair of commas is necessary:

At last, he said, "Thanks for all your help."

"That's all right," we answered. There was an uncomfortable pause.

"Another time," he added, "you can come by yourselves. You only want me as your servant."

If two (or more) sentences are spoken, and separated by 'he said', etc., a full stop is needed:

"Let's change the subject, shall we?" said Jean. "I'm hungry. Let's eat now."

I agreed readily to this suggestion. "I could eat a horse," I said, rather rashly. "It's hours since breakfast."

Mike sat up. "Really? There's one in the next field." He pointed over my shoulder, then continued, "I'll eat your sausage rolls while you catch it."

Add full stops and commas to the following passage, together with capital letters where necessary:

a man selling vacuum cleaners knocked on the door of a remote farmhouse when the farmer's wife opened it the salesman said: "Madam I want to show you something you'll never forget"

Before she could answer he threw a bag of dirt onto her clean floor "Now" he went on "I want to make a bargain with you if the latest model Electrosucks vacuum cleaner doesn't pick up every bit of that dust I'll eat it"

"Here's a spoon" the farmer's wife said "we haven't got electricity"

Add the missing commas to this passage (taken from the opening of *Great Expectations*, by Charles Dickens):

At the same time he hugged his shuddering body in both his arms clasping himself as if to hold himself together and limped towards the low church wall. As I saw him go picking his way among the nettles and among the brambles that bound the green mounds he looked in my young eyes as if he were eluding the hands of the dead people stretching up cautiously out of their graves to get a twist upon his ankle and pull him in.

When he came to the low church wall he got over it like a man whose legs were numbed and stiff and then turned round to look for me. When I saw him turning I set my face towards home and made the best use of my legs. But presently I looked over my shoulder and saw him going on again towards the river still hugging himself in both arms and picking his way with his sore feet among the great stones dropped into the marshes here and there for stepping-places when the rains were heavy or the tide was in.

Now combine each of the following groups of sentences into a single sentence.

Example: Gorillas live in tropical forests. They climb trees in search of food.

Three possible methods of combining these sentences into one are:

Gorillas live in tropical forests, **and they climb/where they climb/climbing** trees in search of food.

It was an awkward moment. He did not quite like it.

He sat there with his back to the blazing logs. He was a very visible object in the light. All about him the darkness of the forest lay like an impenetrable wall.

Then again he became suddenly aware that the person who watched him had returned. That same intent and concentrated gaze as before was fixed upon him where he lay.

He heard no stealthy tread or snapping of dry twigs. The owner of those steady eyes was very close to him. He was probably not a dozen feet away.

For some minutes he sat without stirring a single muscle. Each muscle was ready and alert. He strained his eyes in vain to pierce the darkness. He only succeeded in dazzling his sight with the reflected light.

He shifted his position slowly. He shifted his position cautiously. He shifted his position in order to obtain another angle of vision. His heart gave two big thumps against his ribs. The hair seemed to rise on his scalp with the sense of cold that gave him goose-flesh.

You can compare your method of joining each group of sentences into one with the author's by referring to 1.1.4, where the passage is used for another exercise. You will notice, however, that no commas appear there. You may well have combined the sentences in different ways, but you should have used the comma in the same way, marking the pauses between one section of a sentence and the next (i.e. as in this sentence before 'marking' and 'but').

In the first and third groups of sentences, the author has simply joined them with the conjunction 'and':

It was an awkward moment, **and** he did not quite like it.

Then again he became suddenly aware that the person who watched him had returned, **and** that same . . .

The same word could have been used to link the three sentences in the second group—but that would be very monotonous. Instead, the writer simply leaves out 'He was' when joining the first two sentences:

He sat there with his back to the blazing logs, a very visible object in the light

and links the third sentence with 'while'

. . . in the light, **while** all about him . . .

'He was' is similarly omitted in the fourth group of sentences, while the contrast in the meaning of the first two sentences is shown by linking them with 'yet':

He heard no stealthy tread or snapping of dry twigs, **yet** the owner of those steady eyes was very close to him, probably not a dozen feet away.

In the next group of sentences, the author uses 'yet' again when combining the first two: what other change has been made?

For some minutes he sat without stirring a single muscle, yet with each muscle ready and alert. . . .

The other two sentences in this group are combined into a single, longer sentence by changing the form of the verbs 'strained' and 'succeeded' into the -ing (participle) form (*see* 16) which can be used as a means of linking in the same way as a conjunction:

perhaps you wrote

> . . . ready and alert, **while/, as/, and** he strained his eyes in vain . . .

whereas the author's version is

> . . . ready and alert, straining his eyes in vain to pierce the darkness . . .

The author then uses a conjunction ('but') together with the participle form of the verb ('succeeding')

> . . . to pierce the darkness, **but** only succeed**ing** in . . .

Discuss the ways in which the author combines the final group of sentences into one longer sentence, comparing his version with yours:

> Then, as he shifted his position slowly, cautiously, to obtain another angle of vision, his heart gave two big thumps against his ribs, and the hair seemed to rise on his scalp with the sense of cold that gave him goose-flesh.

Remember that whatever means of linking the sentences you may use, a comma is needed before the linking word.

1.2.2.   Here is Dickens' punctuation of the passage from *Great Expectations* used at the beginning of 1.2.1:

> At the same time, he hugged his shuddering body in both his arms—clasping himself, as if to hold himself together—and limped towards the low church wall. As I saw him go, picking his way among the nettles, and among the brambles that bound the green mounds, he looked in my young eyes as if he were eluding the hands of the dead people, stretching up cautiously out of their graves, to get a twist upon his ankle and pull him in.
>
> When he came to the low church wall, he got over it, like a man whose legs were numbed and stiff, and then turned round to look for me. When I saw him turning, I set my face towards home, and made the best use of my legs. But presently I looked over my shoulder, and saw him going on again towards the river, still hugging himself in both arms, and picking his way with his sore feet among the great stones dropped into the marshes here and there, for stepping-places when the rains were heavy, or the tide was in.

(Dickens uses a pair of dashes instead of commas in the first sentence, separating the group of words between the dashes from the rest of the sentence more sharply than commas would have done)

Compare your punctuation with the above, then add commas to this further extract, taken from the opening of Chapter 3 (Pip, a small boy, has met an escaped convict still wearing leg-irons who has terrified him into stealing a file and food):

> It was a rimy morning and very damp. I had seen the damp lying on the outside of my little window as if some goblin had been crying there all night and using the window for a pocket-handkerchief. Now I saw the damp lying on the bare hedges and spare grass like a coarser sort of spider's web hanging itself from twig to twig and blade to blade. . . .
>
> The mist was heavier yet when I got out upon the marshes so that instead of my running at everything everything seemed to run at me. This was very disagreeable to a guilty mind. The gates and dykes and banks came bursting at me through the mist as if they cried as plainly as could be "A boy with somebody-else's pork pie! Stop him!" The cattle came upon me with like suddenness staring out of their eyes and steaming out of their nostrils "Holloa young thief!"
>
> All this time I was getting on toward the river but however fast I went I couldn't warm my feet to which the damp cold seemed riveted as the iron was riveted to the leg of the man I was running to meet.

1.2.3   The picnic hamper was lent to us by Mike's uncle. It was quite heavy.

The picnic hamper (which Mike's uncle lent us) was quite heavy.

The picnic hamper, which Mike's uncle lent us, was quite heavy.

Mike is strong for his age. Mike carried it by himself.

Mike (who is strong for his age) carried it by himself.

Mike, who is strong for his age, carried it by himself.

In the above examples, two sentences have been combined into one by using a pair of commas as if they were brackets. The two sentences are about the same subject (the picnic hamper in the first example, Mike in the second) and are closely related in meaning, so it makes sense to join them together. *Do the same with the following pairs of sentences. Start each combined sentence with its subject, then add a comma:*

Gorillas,
The picnic hamper,
Mike,

Next add the information from one of the original sentences about the subject
(Gorillas) live in tropical forests
(The picnic hamper) was lent to us by Mike's uncle
(Mike) is strong for his age

showing the relation between it and the subject by using a relative pronoun (who, which).
Gorillas, which live in tropical forests
The picnic hamper, which was lent to us by Mike's uncle
Mike, who is strong for his age

Now add the second comma, to keep the two parts of your combined sentence separate, and the remainder of the other original sentence:
Gorillas, which live in tropical forests, climb trees in search of food.
The picnic hamper, which was lent to us by Mike's uncle, was quite heavy.
Mike, who is strong for his age, carried it by himself.

Her uncle is looking for a house. He has been promoted. The house must be situated within easy reach of the city centre. It should be able to accommodate a family of five.

The three children are noisy and tend to quarrel. They need separate bedrooms.

A house for sale in Park Road would appear to be ideal for them. It has four bedrooms and a large garden.

The house used to be owned by a retired builder. It is in good repair.

The house is very comfortable. It has full central heating, a fully-equipped kitchen, and plenty of built-in cupboards and wardrobes.

Her uncle and aunt have had the house surveyed. They can find no fault with it.

1.2.4   Two or more sentences can be combined using the method shown in 1.2.3, and in other ways (illustrated in 1.2.1), for instance, by using:
a conjunction, e.g. 'and', 'but', 'so'
a relative pronoun, e.g. 'who', 'which', 'that'
a participle form of a verb, e.g. The children screamed, **terrified** by the monster.

If the linking word comes in the middle of the combined sentence, it follows a comma:
Examples

Mike carried the picnic hamper by himself, **since** he is strong for his age.

Mike carried the picnic hamper by himself, **being** strong for his age.

Mike's uncle lent us his picnic hamper, **which** was very kind of him, **but** it was rather heavy.

It was kind of Mike's uncle to lend us his picnic hamper, **though** it was rather heavy.

The first of these examples could have been written in a different order:

Since he is strong for his age, Mike carried the picnic hamper by himself.

Although the linking word is now at the beginning of the sentence, note how the comma remains to mark the pause between the two parts.
Similarly,

Being strong for his age, Mike carried the picnic hamper by himself.

Look carefully at the punctuation of these further examples:

Puffing and snorting, Mike lay down. He lay there for some time, stretched out on the grass, not saying a word. He looked up at the clouds, scowling.

The sun was shining brightly, but in the west clouds were gathering. Soon a strong breeze developed into a gale-force wind, so we packed the hamper again. Then we ran back down the hill, leaving Mike to bring the hamper. When he caught up with us at the bus stop, the drizzle was turning into rain.

How many different ways can you find to join these sentences into one?
Underline the linking words, **and** *the commas you put before them*

The thief rushed out of the room.

The thief was terrified in case he might be caught.

The thief did not notice an open trapdoor.

The thief fell through the trapdoor into a cellar full of coal.

The thief was pursued by a detective.

The order of the sentences, and the words in them, can be altered, and there is no need to restrict yourself to using the words only in the forms used here: for instance, 'terror' and 'capture' could be used instead of 'terrified' and 'in case he might be caught'.

When combining sentences, make sure that the links you use don't cause confusion! *For example, how would you re-phrase and punctuate these sentences to make their meaning more clear?*

Crossing the road the church seemed much bigger than previously.

He looked at the church again after crossing the road which seemed much bigger than previously.

He crossed the road which ran alongside the church without noticing a large puddle.

He was going to the cinema which was showing a film about Dracula after a check-up at the dentist's.

Combine the following pairs or groups of sentences:

Derek Ware is a stuntman. He prefers to call himself 'a specialist in hazards.' He stands in for the stars during the dangerous bits of a film.

He specializes in swordplay and horsemanship. He's prepared to undertake most assignments.

One day he was working on a sequence for a TV film. The sequence followed a car chase. The car chase came to an end when a helicopter landed besides the villain's vehicle.

A few days earlier he had injured his shoulder. He had been standing in for a character. The character was supposed to be punched on the jaw. The impact sent the character tumbling down the stairs.

For a spectacular but 'safe' fall, stairs should be as steep as possible. This particular flight was not steep enough.

Derek Ware smashed his shoulder on the banister rail. He tore a muscle. For some time afterwards he could not raise the arm.

He had been contracted to perform his next stunt in a few days' time. He could not let the director down.

He was treated by a physiotherapist. He did many exercises. Some injuries can only be healed by time.

The villain was to enter the helicopter. The helicopter then took off.

The machine was still a few feet off the ground. The hero was supposed to climb on to the roof of his car. He was supposed to grab hold of the helicopter's undercarriage. He was then to be hauled into the sky.

The car set off at twenty-five miles an hour. The pilot of the helicopter kept pace with it.

Derek Ware grabbed hold of one of the struts. The pilot soared up thirty feet. Derek Ware could not raise his injured arm high enough to reach the strut. He found himself suspended in mid-air beneath the helicopter. He was hanging on by only one hand.

He lost his grip on the strut. He fell down on to the roof of the car. He bounced off on to the bonnet. He bounced off the bonnet on to the ground.

He suffered cuts and bruises on his face and six cracked ribs. He had fallen thirty feet. His injuries might have been fatal if he had missed the car.

The producer ran out of money. The film was never finished. The helicopter sequence was shown. It was shown in a TV documentary. The documentary featured the work of stuntmen.

1.2.5   *Expand the following notes into sentences separated by full stops. (There is no need to write a new sentence for each new piece of information given: sometimes you may wish to join two or more notes into one sentence, using joining words and commas as in 1.2.4.)*
Girl went to race meeting—proud of new engagement ring—worth £350—loose—fell off finger—not noticed by girl until later in afternoon—hysterical—loss reported to police—thorough search—unsuccessful. Fortnight later girl's mother went to same racecourse—at end of race meeting returned to car—noticed something twinkling on ground —daughter's ring—undamaged

1.2.6   *Imagine you are a newspaper reporter. You have been assigned to 'cover' three stories concerning animals. Below are your notes taken when telephoning your contacts. Use them to write brief summaries for your sub-editor, so that he can choose which story to expand into a news feature (with interviews, photographs, etc.). For each story write a single paragraph, making sure that these notes become complete sentences.*
St Oswald's Church, Ashton—Goat (named Oswald)—

bought four years ago to keep graveyard tidy—now grown too fat to manœuvre between gravestones—problem—redundant, but what to do with him?

Kensington, London—man found snake on kitchen window ledge—5 feet long West African royal python—flat four storeys above street level—London Zoo spokesman asked for possible explanation—snake probably escaped pet—sunning itself on roof of flats.

Sudbury, Suffolk—Mill Hotel—four years ago building contractor discovered mummified black cat under floorboards—buried centuries ago by superstitious local people who believed it would ward off fire—removed by contractor who was making alterations to the Hotel—since then two fires and a subsiding wall—contractor thinks they were caused by his tampering with fate—now renovating the Hotel—owners have ordered return of body to its previous grave under floor.

(You will find one newspaper's versions of these stories in 2.3.3.)

1.2.7   *Imagine you work for an advertising agency. A leading car manufacturer is launching a new model on the market and has provided you with the following list of specifications. Use these notes as the basis for a description of the car for inclusion in the brochure that will be distributed to retailers throughout the country. The illustrations and accompanying captions have been decided on already: your brief is to write a fuller account of the car that will tell the prospective buyer what its main features are, drawing attention especially to its safety, fuel economy, comfort and power. Write your account simply and clearly: this will mean re-arranging the notes into a more sensible order (for instance, collecting all the details that emphasize the car's safety features) before you turn them into sentences arranged in paragraphs.*

11 versions: 2-door, 4-door, 5-door estate standard and Special + choice of two power units – 1300 and 1600. Wide choice of optional extras.

Seats built generously. Soft. Enveloping. Widest car in its category.

Performance: 1600 cc ohv engine gives max 96 mph (155 km/h). Acceleration 0–60 13 sec.

Capacity: 5 persons + 50 kg luggage

Safety body shell—3 horizontal protective structures running round body at floor and roof levels and in middle of doors.

Child-proof locks on rear doors (prevent doors from being opened from inside)

Anti-rust underbody protection: underside of body shell,

wheel arches and lower body sills have thick layer of PVC
Adjustable steering wheel, heated rear screen, reclining front
seats, reversing lights standard
Fuel consumption: 27–30 mpg on 4-star petrol. 11 gal.
tank—280 miles.
Bumpers can retract 6 cm without damaging bodywork
Padded roof for better heat/sound insulation—one-piece
expanded polyurethane panel 2 cm thick
Fuel tank located behind rear seat backrest—area most
protected from impact. Also steel bulkhead isolates passenger
from luggage compartment
Dual independent brake circuits
Central electrical control box under dashboard. Combines
relays, fuses, and three multiple sockets which link entire
electrical system
Bolt-on front wings—easy to replace in event of damage
Non-reflective instrument lights, illuminated cigarette
lighter/ashtray
Excellent visibility—large glass area/slim pillars

1.2.8   *Imagine you are compiling a cookery book. Use the following notes as the basis
for a recipe that will give clear instructions for making short crust pastry:*
      200 g flour   good pinch salt   50 g margarine   50 g
cooking fat   approx 2 tablespoons cold water to mix
Sieve flour/salt together
Rub in marg./fat till mixture looks like fine breadcrumbs
Gradually add enough cold water to make dough rolling
consistency
Use knife first, then fingertips
Lightly flour rolling pin, pastry board
Roll pastry to required thickness, shape
Lift and turn pastry while rolling—to keep light
Hot oven (425–450°F/gas mark 6–7) till golden brown

1.3.1   I stole some bread, some rind of cheese, about half a jar of
mincemeat, some brandy from a stone bottle, a meat bone
with very little on it, and a beautiful round compact pork pie.

Commas are used to separate items in a list. *Add the commas needed in
the following recipe:*
      For four people you will need the following ingredients: 100 g
shortcrust pastry 1 packet lemon pie filling 300 ml water 1
small lemon 3 eggs and 150 g caster sugar. To begin roll out
the pastry line a greased 8-inch round flan tin (or Pyrex pie

dish) with it prick the bottom all over with a fork and bake it for about 30 minutes at gas mark 4 (350°F.). For the filling separate the eggs beat the yolks and put them in a saucepan together with the pie filling the juice and grated rind of the lemon and 300 ml of water. Bring to the boil whisking with a balloon whisk to prevent lumps and let it boil for a minute or two until thick. Now whisk the whites till they form peaks and gradually beat in the sugar a tablespoonful at a time. Pour the lemon filling into the pastry case then top with the meringue mixture making sure it covers all the filling and seal it in round the edges. Bake in a slow oven at gas mark 2 (300°F.) for 30 minutes

(Delia Smith, *Evening Standard Cookery Book*)

Now add commas to these descriptions:

I saw the rust-brown face a gaunt Indian nose and smelt a reek of cigars and train-oil. Here was the hero of our school-boasting days and to look on him was no disappointment. He was shiny as iron worn as a rock and lay like a chieftain sleeping. . . . With his leather-beaten face wide teeth-crammed mouth and far-seeing ice-blue eyes he looked like some wigwam warrior stained with suns and heroic slaughter. . . . His body was tattooed in every quarter—ships in full sail flags of all nations reptiles and round-eyed maidens. By cunning flexings of his muscles he could sail these ships wave the flags in the wind and coil snakes round the quivering girls.

(Laurie Lee, *Cider With Rosie*)

But there he was always a steaming hulk of an uncle his braces straining like hawsers crammed behind the counter of the tiny shop at the front of the house and breathing like a brass band; or guzzling and blustery in the kitchen over his gutsy supper too big for everything except the great black boats of his boots. As he ate the house grew smaller; he billowed out over the furniture the loud check meadow of his waistcoat littered as though after a picnic with cigarette ends peelings cabbage stalks birds' bones gravy. . . .

(Dylan Thomas, *A Prospect of the Sea*)

1.3.2   For four people you will need the following ingredients:
Add the commas needed in the following descriptions:
The following items had to be packed: plates, cups, kettles, bottles, jars, pies, stoves, cakes, tomatoes.

A colon (:) can be used to introduce a list. *Using colons and commas, list the following:*

the sounds around you

what there is to be seen through the nearest window

the main features of the room in which you are working

1.3.3 *Use the following notes as the basis for a description of a car:*
4-speed all-syncromesh gearbox
front-wheel drive
independent torsion bar suspension
rack and pinion steering   —give driver relaxed sense of
disc/drum brakes   being in complete control

hooded instrument panel houses:
speedometer
mileage recorder
fuel gauge
+warning lights for choke/direction indicators/oil pressure/
water temperature
to right of instrument panel:
rocker switches for heated rear window
two-speed heater fan
two separate angled vents to direct air onto side windows
to right of steering column:
lights
horn
headlamps
headlamp flashers
direction indicators—controlled by two levers
to left of steering column:
fingertip switch
for electric windscreen washer
two-speed wipers
(lower down) bonnet release
to left of instrument panel:
face-level main fresh air vent
(below) heater controls, ashtray
choke control on extreme right

room to stretch for 4 large adults
plenty of head/leg/elbow room front and back
no transmission tunnel occupying valuable floor space
luxury equipment included in basic price:
heater and demister with electric booster fan
fresh-air vents

interior courtesy lights
headlamp flasher
twin sun visors
two-speed electric windscreen wipers
electrically-operated windscreen washers
anti-theft steering lock
heated rear window
front/rear parcel shelves
vanity mirror
ashtrays
arm rests
passenger grab-handles

all steel construction
easily replaceable bolt-on wings
bumper shields absorb impacts of up to 5 mph without
    distortion
whole body dipped to waist level in anti-corrosive paint
rust-inhibitor/anti-freeze sealed in cooling system
cooling system has thermostatically-controlled fan
no greasing points—maintenance minimal

$9\frac{1}{2}$ cubic feet boot
(spare wheel/jack kept under bonnet)
with parcel shelf lowered room for large awkward objects
—e.g. large dog
for more space:
tip forward rear bench seat
release two catches holding back rest in position—estate
car with firm level floor + 32 cubic feet of space
large objects easily loaded through wide counter-balanced
    tailgate (opens to floor level)
headlamps can be adjusted for height at flick of switch
    according to load being carried

1.3.4   *Imagine you are compiling a new Highway Code. Give advice to motorists
on parking, using the following notes:*
        Do not park or let your vehicle stand:
        —where see these signs (no parking/clearway/yellow lines
            beside kerb/double white lines in middle of road)
        —where it would make it difficult for others to see clearly (i.e.
            junction/bend/brow of hill/hump-back bridge/level
            crossing)
        —where danger to other road users (bus stop/pedestrian
            crossing/school entrance/footpath, pavement, cycle
            path/right-hand side of street at night/hiding traffic sign)

—where cause traffic to be held up/inconvenience (narrow road/flyovers, tunnels, underpasses/fast main roads —except lay-by/motorways—except hard shoulder in emergency/single track road/outside private entrance)
—where emergency vehicles stop/go in/go out
—where would make road narrow (e.g. near road works, alongside another parked vehicle/etc.)

1.3.5   *Punctuate the following description of a chase:*
"Stop thief! Stop thief!' There is a magic in the sound the tradesman leaves his counter and the carman his waggon the butcher throws down his tray the baker his basket the milkman his pail the errand-boy his parcels the school-boy his marbles the paviour his pick-axe the child his battledore away they run pell-mell helter-skelter slap-dash tearing yelling screaming knocking down the passengers as they turn the corners rousing up the dogs and astonishing the fowls streets squares and courts re-echo with the sound
   stop thief stop thief the cry is taken up by a hundred voices and the crowd accumulate at every turning away they fly splashing through the mud and rattling along the pavements up go the windows out run the people onward bear the mob a whole audience desert Punch in the very thickest of the plot and joining the rushing throng swell the shout and lend fresh vigour to the cry stop thief stop thief
   stop thief stop thief there is a passion for hunting something deeply implanted in the human breast one wretched breathless child panting with exhaustion terror in his looks agony in his eyes large drops of perspiration streaming down his face strains every nerve to make head upon his pursuers and as they follow on his track and gain upon him every instant they hail his decreasing strength with still louder shouts and whoop and scream with joy stop thief stop thief ay stop him for God's sake were it only in mercy
                  (Charles Dickens, *Oliver Twist*, chapter 10)

In the first paragraph, the writer separates the items in the first list by semi-colons (;): 'the tradesman leaves his counter, and the carman his waggon; the butcher throws down his tray; the baker his basket; . . .' and so on until . . . 'the child his battledore'. The next list is separated by commas: 'pell-mell, helter-skelter, slap-dash, tearing, yelling, screaming . . .'
   Semi-colons can be used in this way to separate long and rather complicated items in a complicated list. Can you find instances in

subsequent paragraphs in the above description where semi-colons would be preferable to commas?

1.3.6   *Punctuate the following description, using full stops, commas, and semi-colons where appropriate:*

the first shock of a great earthquake had just at that period rent the whole neighbourhood to its centre traces of its course were visible on every side houses were knocked down streets broken through and stopped deep pits and trenches dug in the ground enormous heaps of earth and clay thrown up buildings that were undermined and shaking propped by great beams of wood here a chaos of carts overthrown and jumbled together lay topsy-turvy at the bottom of a steep unnatural hill there confused treasures of iron soaked and rusted in something that had accidentally become a pond everywhere were bridges that led nowhere Babel towers of chimneys wanting half their height temporary wooden houses and enclosures in the most unlikely situations carcases of ragged tenements and fragments of unfinished walls and arches and piles of scaffolding and wildernesses of bricks and giant forms of cranes and tripods straddling above nothing there were a hundred thousand shapes and substances of incompleteness wildly mingled out of their places upside down burrowing in the earth aspiring in the air mouldering in the water and unintelligible as any dream hot springs and fiery eruptions the usual attendants upon earthquakes lent their contributions of confusion to the scene boiling water hissed and heaved within dilapidated walls whence also the glare and roar of flames came issuing forth and mounds of ashes blocked up rights of way and wholly changed the law and custom of the neighbourhood

in short, the yet unfinished and unopened Railroad was in progress. . . .

(Charles Dickens, *Dombey and Son*, chapter 6)

1.3.7   *Write an account of causes of accidents in the home, using the following notes:*
Falls—badly designed houses   poor lighting (esp. stair-cases/passages)   highly polished floors   worn/wrinkled floor coverings/slip mats on polished floors   worn stair coverings loose stair rods   steep staircases/inadequate rails trailing flex   spilt grease   obstacles left on stairs/elsewhere (toys, domestic equipment)   chairs too low   slippery baths (esp. dangerous to elderly)   high chairs/prams for young with inadequate harnesses   un-

guarded windows/stairs   beds too high from floor   over-reaching on ladders/steps   standing on chairs to reach high places/hang curtains   making do without a light unsuitable—if fashionable—footwear

Burns—contact with unguarded fires (e.g. open coal, gas, electric)   oil-burning stoves accidents   inflammable fabrics—winceyette/flannelette/many synthetic fabrics wearing long, loose garments (esp. nightwear) made of these fabrics   use of cleaning solvents like petrol indoors——naked lights/burning cigarettes

Scalds—chiefly affect toddlers

hot water—falling into hot washingwater/scrubbing water left on floor, playing with washing machines

cooking—overturning saucepans (handles left sticking out over stove)   pulling leads to electric kettles   pulling drapes of table cloths with teapots etc. on them   knocking over cups of tea when being nursed   steam from kettle bathing—hotwater put into bath before cold   bath water too hot   unprotected hot water bottles   hot water bottles left in baby's bed when put to sleep

Poisoning—town gas—leaks/inadequate ventilation/children tampering with gas taps/blocked flue outlets on gas appliances medicinal—drugs (esp. tablets) left within reach of children children eating rubs/creams/lotions/powders prescribed for external use only   persons taking wrong substances from unlabelled bottles/overdoses from absent-mindedness, wrong medicine

household—chemicals/gardening fluids taken by error (often resemble soft drinks)   drinking of substances in unlabelled bottles/wrongly labelled (e.g. soft drink label from original use)

Suffocation—chiefly tragedy of babies   pillow too large/soft   overlaying (taken into adults' bed—rolled on/trapped between two adults)   failure to tuck in bedclothes/wrapping baby too tightly   by inhalation—propping bottle in baby's mouth, allowing to feed itself, putting baby to rest too soon after feed without bringing up its wind, placing on its back (any food brought up cannot be released without choking child)   smothering by cat (etc.) sleeping in cot/pram containing a child

1.3.8   *Give clear directions on the following operations, so that they can be followed safely by a person who is unfamiliar with them:*

wiring a three-pin plug for a domestic appliance
changing a wheel after a car has had a puncture—on a bend

first aid for a person who has been knocked down by a vehicle and is unconscious, or who appears to have drowned

advice on making a 999 call after a fire

advice to motorists when overtaking

advice to cyclists/motorists when turning right, at a road junction, and at a roundabout

advice to young children on how to cross roads safely

directions for the easiest route for a person travelling from your college to your home

advice on a nutritious and economical meal for a person living alone—including how to prepare it.

1.4.1   A colon can be used to introduce a list (*see 1.3.2*). It can also be used after a statement in order to introduce some additional information:

The musket was already something of an antique: it had changed very little in the past 150 years.

Musketry and artillery were only useful in the mass: if you fired a big enough volley, some of the shots would probably hit the target. If you yourself were shot on the battlefield, it was highly unlikely that the shot had been aimed at you as an individual: the risk was mainly from the quantity of shot which aimlessly flew around from the tens of thousands of weapons. So the Duke could ride up and down observing the enemy, and in full view of them: he ran a great risk of being shot, but very little risk from being deliberately shot at.

(David Howarth, *A Near-Run Thing*)

Add colons at the appropriate points in the following sentences:

The reason I made no comment was quite simple when George is hanged Harris will be the worst packer in the world.

When George is hanged Harris will be the worst packer in the world that is why I made no comment, but just waited.

I don't know how it is, but I never do know whether I've packed my toothbrush in the middle of the night I dream that I haven't packed it, wake up in a cold perspiration, get out of bed and hunt for it.

This is what happens in the morning I pack it before I've used it, and have to unpack again to get it, finding it's always the last thing I turn out of the bag.

In the morning I pack it before I've used it and have to unpack again to get it it's always the last thing I turn out of the bag.

In the above examples, each statement you have separated by a colon makes complete sense by itself: it is a sentence. A colon is thus being used as an alternative to a full stop: the statement following it gives further information about the preceding one. A comma would have been too weak a pause to separate them: a joining-word, or the participle form of the verb would have been necessary also (*see 1.1.3*), as is shown in the last example but one—

   ... and have to unpack again to get it, **finding** it's always the last thing I turn out of the bag.

A colon is a sophisticated means of separating sentences: if in doubt, always use a full stop, never a comma by itself.

How could you combine the other sentences you have divided by colons?

Punctuate the following passage, using commas, full stops, and colons as an alternative to full stops where appropriate:

   Among Wellington's own men the ecstasy of the review was fading and the cheering had died away among the British and their allies or at least among those who had heard that the Prussians were coming surprise at his inactivity was growing for them the longer he put it off the better all over the field men stood silent in their ranks or sat on the ground in desultory conversation or lay dozing with their heads on their knapsacks after the cold wet night everyone was grateful for the sun a kind of peace a sense of lethargy descended and men's thoughts strayed away to happier scenes and people far away mothers lovers and homes old soldiers told boastful stories to new recruits who did not want to listen it began to be hard to believe that the calm of the summer's day would be broken yet everyone knew there was no retreat that before the sun went down there must be slaughter and chaos in the quiet fields men's spirits sank with the waiting and they secretly looked at each other and wondered which would die but whatever his private feelings nobody could admit he was afraid all of those thousands of patient men had one thing in common each of them understood his own weapon and more or less understood the battle drill and tactics of using it

1.4.2   They began in a light-hearted spirit, evidently intending to show me how to do it. I made no comment; I only waited. When George is hanged Harris will be the worst packer in the world; and I looked at the piles of plates, and cups, and kettles, and bottles, and jars, and pies, and stoves, and cakes, and tomatoes, etc., and felt that the thing would soon become exciting.

Semi-colons (;) can be used as an alternative to commas when separating items in a complicated list (see 1.3.5); and they can also be used as an alternative when combining two sentences with a conjunction ('and', 'but', etc.) into one, as in this sentence and in the sentence above beginning 'When George is hanged. . .'. They can also be used, like colons, as an alternative to full stops, linking sentences that are closely connected in sense into one larger sentence. Again, in the example above, a comma would be insufficient to mark the pause, needing a conjunction or the participle form of the verb as well:

I made no comment; I only waited.

I made no comment, *but* only waited.

I made no comment, merely *waiting*.

I waited, *making* no comment.

I waited, *and* made no comment.

I waited, *without making* any comment.

I waited; I made no comment.

Insert semi-colons at appropriate points in the following sentences:

Like all birds of prey, the kestrel is protected by law throughout the year but unlike many of the others, it is not in desperate need of this protection. Farmers recognize the bird as a useful ally against mice, rats, voles and harmful insects and enlightened gamekeepers are prepared to overlook the occasional gamechick it takes because of its value as a destroyer of pests. Partly because it does not have to face persecution, and partly because it can adapt to many different kinds of country, the kestrel has become by far the commonest of Britain's day-flying birds of prey it is equally at home in farmland, moorland and along sea-cliffs. In recent years it has become very much an urban bird, too in central London, its nesting places have included a tower in the House of Lords. Its hovering flight, with tail fanned out and wings flapping vigorously as it watches the ground for voles and mice, is also a familiar sight along motorway verges.

Recognition: pointed wings and long tail male has blue-grey head, rump and tail, with black band at end of tail female has barred tail, also with black band hovering flight is distinctive.

Feeding: mainly mice, voles, and young rats also frogs, earthworms and insects sparrows and other birds in towns.

Add commas and semi-colons to the following passage:

A large cask of wine had been dropped and broken in the street. The accident had happened in getting it out of a cart the cask had tumbled out with a run the hoops had burst and it lay on the stones just outside the door of the wine-shop shattered like a walnut-shell.

All the people within reach had suspended their business or their idleness to run to the spot and drink the wine. The rough irregular stones of the street pointing every way and designed one might have thought expressly to lame all living creatures that approached them had dammed it into little pools these were surrounded each by its own jostling group or crowd according to its size. Some men kneeled down made scoops of their two hands joined and sipped or tried to help women who bent over their shoulders to sip before the wine had all run out between their fingers. Other men and women dipped in the puddles with little mugs of mutilated earthenware or even with handkerchiefs from women's heads which were squeezed dry into infants' mouths others made small mud-embankments to stem the wine as it ran others directed by lookers-on up at high windows darted here and there to cut off little streams of wine that started away in new directions others devoted themselves to the sodden and lee-dyed pieces of the cask licking and even champing the moister wine-rotted fragments with eager relish. There was no drainage to carry off the wine and not only did it all get taken up but so much mud got taken up along with it that there might have been a scavenger in the street if anybody acquainted with it could have believed in such a miraculous presence.

A shrill sound of laughter and of amused voices of men women and children resounded in the street while this wine game lasted. There was little roughness in the sport and much playfulness. There was a special companionship in it an observable inclination on the part of every one to join some other one which led especially among the luckier or light-hearted to frolicsome embraces drinking of healths shaking of hands and even joining of hands and dancing a dozen together. When the wine was gone and the places where it had been most abundant were raked into a gridiron-pattern by fingers these demonstrations ceased as suddenly as they had broken out. The man who had left his saw sticking in the firewood he was cutting set it in motion again the woman who had left on a door-step the little pot of hot ashes at which she had been trying to soften the pain in her own starved fingers and toes or in those of her child returned to it men with bare arms matted locks and cadaverous faces who had emerged

31

into the winter light from cellars moved away to descend again and a gloom gathered on the scene that appeared more natural to it than sunshine.

The wine was red wine and had stained the ground of the narrow street in the suburb of Saint Antoine in Paris where it had spilled. It had stained many hands too and many faces and many naked feet and many wooden shoes. The hands of the man who sawed the wood left red marks on the billets and the forehead of the woman who nursed her baby was stained with the stain of the old rag she wound about her head again. Those who had been greedy with the staves of the cask had acquired a tigerish smear about the mouth and one tall joker so besmirched his head more out of a long squalid bag of a nightcap than in it scrawled upon a wall with his finger dipped in muddy wine-lees—BLOOD.

(Charles Dickens, *A Tale of Two Cities*, opening of chapter 5)

1.4.4   *Punctuate the following passage (which continues from where the passage in 1.1.3 ends), using commas, full stops, and semi-colons where you wish to emphasize the connection in meaning between two sentences:*

Gradually there came a sort of vague beginning of consciousness then a sense of weariness that was dreadful for a time I remembered nothing but slowly my senses returned my feet seemed positively racked with pain yet I could not move them they seemed to be numbed there was an icy feeling at the back of my neck and all down my spine and my ears like my feet were dead yet in torment but there was in my breast a sense of warmth which was by comparison delicious it was as a nightmare a physical nightmare if one may use such an expression for some heavy weight on my chest made it difficult for me to breathe

This period of semi-lethargy seemed to remain a long time and as it faded away I must have slept or swooned then came a sort of loathing like the first stage of seasickness and a wild desire to be free of something I knew not what a vast stillness enveloped me as though all the world were asleep or dead only broken by the low panting as of some animal close to me I felt a warm rasping at my throat then came a consciousness of the awful truth which chilled me to the heart and sent the blood surging up through my brain some great animal was lying on me and now licking my throat I feared to stir for some instinct of prudence bade me lie still but the brute seemed to realize that there was now some change in me for it raised its head through my eyelashes I saw above me the two great flaming eyes of a gigantic wolf its sharp white teeth

gleamed in the gaping red mouth and I could feel its hot
breath fierce and acrid upon me.

1.4.5 *Combine the following list of sentences into paragraphs that will give a*
connected description of this episode in Three Men In A Boat. *Sometimes*
the sentences can be left as they are. At other times, you may wish to change
their order, and combine them into longer sentences (thus altering their
wording—adding conjunctions to show the connection between sentences,
changing the verb form, substituting pronouns for nouns, etc.).

We tackled the cold beef for lunch
We found that we had forgotten to bring any mustard
It cast a gloom over the boat, there being no mustard
We ate our beef in silence
Existence seemed hollow and uninteresting
We thought of the happy days of childhood
We sighed
We brightened up a bit, however, over the apple tart
George drew out a tin of pineapple from the bottom of the
hamper
George rolled a tin of pineapple to the middle of the boat
We felt that life was worth living after all

We are very fond of pineapple, all three of us
We looked at the picture on the tin
We thought of the juice
We smiled at one another
Harris got a spoon ready

We looked for the knife to open the tin with
We turned out everything in the hamper
We turned out the bags
We pulled up the boards at the bottom of the boat
We took everything out on to the bank and shook it
There was no tin-opener to be found

Harris tried to open the tin with a pocket-knife
Harris broke the knife
Harris cut himself badly
George tried a pair of scissors
The scissors flew up
The scissors nearly put his eye out
They were dressing their wounds
I tried to make a hole in the tin with the spiky end of the
hitcher
The hitcher slipped and jerked me out between the boat and
the bank into two feet of muddy water

The tin rolled over, uninjured
The tin broke a teacup

We all got mad
We took that tin out on the bank
Harris went up into a field and got a big sharp stone
I went back into the boat and brought out the mast
George held the tin
Harris held the sharp end of his stone against the top of it
I took the mast and poised it high up in the air
I gathered up all my strength and brought it down

It was George's straw hat that saved his life that day
He keeps that hat now (what is left of it)
Of a winter's evening, when the pipes are lit George shows it round
The stirring tale is told anew, with fresh exaggerations every time

Harris got off merely with a flesh wound
I took the tin off by myself
I hammered at the tin with the mast till I was worn out and sick at heart
Harris took it in hand

We beat it out flat
We beat it back square
We battered it into every form known to geometry
We could not make a hole in it
George went at it
George knocked it into a shape, so strange, so weird, so unearthly in its wild hideousness
George got frightened and threw away the mast
We all three sat round it on the grass and looked at it

There was one dent across the top
The dent had the appearance of a mocking grin
The mocking grin drove us furious
Harris rushed at the thing
Harris caught the thing up
Harris flung the thing far into the middle of the river
It sank
We hurled our curses at it
We got into the boat
We rowed away from the spot
We never paused till we reached Maidenhead

1.4.6 *Expand these notes into a newspaper article. Put the points into a sensible order, write complete sentences, and connect them into paragraphs. When your article is written, complete it with a headline that will arouse the reader's interest.*

Moveable bathtub (Holland). Hospitals/invalids. Adjustable height: 51–102 cm above floor (i.e. patient gets in, nurse raises to height most comfortable for bathing patient).

Tokyo—electronic device to tell bus queues how long to wait: radio transmitters on buses, data to computer, electronic message to bus-stop.

Inflatable yacht (Devon)—Tinker Tamborine (30 × 140 × 67·5 cm when packed) fits easily into boot of car, 20 mins to inflate.

All-plastic cycle (weighs 7·2 kilos—most cycles 112·51–157·5) —wheels/frame/handlebars made of polycarbon resin. No oiling, no rust, no chipped paint.

Pneumatic patient-turner (American) for heavy, bedridden patients.

Radio-controlled irrigation system (American) for large lawns/farms/golf courses/parks. Battery-operated. Central control station transmits coded radio signals to satellite stations (set times for this)—these operate motor opening valves to sprinkler heads (pre-determined periods).

Aerosol can containing liquid rubber under pressure—cycle punctures. Connect can to tyre valve—seals puncture automatically, reinflates tyre in less than a minute.

Car radar set (American) should cost no more than car radio, could be mass-produced in next 5 years. Calculates distance between two cars and speeds. Transmitter-receiver on front bumper continually emitting radar signals/passive radar reflector on rear bumper of car in front bounces signals back. At pre-determined distance device automatically causes brakes to be applied.

2 Punctuation—apostrophe, quotation marks

2.1.1   I don't know how it is, but I never do know whether I've packed my toothbrush. When I'm travelling I dream that I haven't packed it and wake up in a cold perspiration, and get out of bed and hunt for it. In the morning I pack it before I've used it, and have to unpack again to get it; and it's always the last thing I turn out of the bag.

The apostrophe (') is used to mark missing letters. Write the shortened form of these phrases, using an apostrophe to mark the place from which you have omitted letters:

I am	
I shall	shall not
I should	should not
you are	are not
you will	will not
you would	would not
we are	
we shall	
we should	
they are	
they will	
they would	
who is	
who would	
it is	is not
that is	
what is	
there is	
	was not
	were not
I have	have not
	has not
	had not

2.1.2   Then it was George's turn. His friend's attempts had included packing the strawberry jam on top of a tomato and squashing it. The hamper's contents were in a terrible mess.
The friends' combined efforts gave me two hours' fun. They weren't so amused.

In the above example, "weren't" = "were not". The other apostrophes are being used for a different purpose—to show that whatever follows the word with the apostrophe belongs to that word. Thus "George's turn" = "the turn of George"; "His friend's attempts" = "the attempts of his friend"; "The hamper's contents" = "The contents of the hamper"; "The friends' combined efforts" = "The combined efforts of the friends"; and "two hours' fun" = "the fun of two hours".

N.B. 1 If the word to which something belongs is singular (one), add 's:
   cat = cat's; lady = lady's; tree = tree's; man = man's;
   child = child's
2 If the word to which something belongs is plural (more than one) and ends in s add the ' only:
   cats = cats'; ladies = ladies'; trees = trees'
3 If the word to which something belongs is plural, but does not end in s, add 's:
   children = children's; men = men's; sheep = sheep's

Re-write the following, using apostrophes:
   the branches of the tree
   the mother of the children
   the shade of the trees
   the Institute of Women
   (the shop) of the grocer
   (the shop) of the hairdresser
   hairdressing for ladies
   in the time of twenty minutes
   the sisters of the child
   the committee of students
   the discussion of two hours

2.1.3   Confusion is often caused by the following:
   it's = it is   its = of it
   there's = there is   theirs = of them
   Susan's = of Susan *or* Susan is—depending on the meaning of the rest of the sentence
   but

37

hers=of her   his=of him   ours=of us   yours=of you
theirs=of them
—no apostrophe

Add apostrophes to the punctuation of the following sentences:
Theres Susans dog. Look—its chasing its tail!
Is it hers or her brothers?
Im not certain whose it is—but its theirs, not their parents.
Yes, the Smiths menagerie isnt too popular with their
neighbours.
They arent very good at keeping them under control.
Who—the children or their animals?
Well, both really. I mean, Mr Smiths always on night shifts
these days, while his wifes always at the hairdressers, so the
childrens time is their own. They seem to run wild most of the
time, just like their pets.
Its criminal, really. You shouldnt have pets if you cant be
bothered to take proper care of them.
The same goes for parents care of their children.
One of these days therell be an accident, wont there?
Wasnt there something in last weeks paper about stray dogs?
Theyve appointed a dog-catcher for the council, I think. Hes
going to have his time taken up catching the Smiths, I
shouldnt wonder.

Wed better hurry or well be late for the six o clock bus.
The buses are usually late, though, arent they?
Well, ours often is. The drivers too busy most of the time
chatting to bother about taking his passengers fares, let alone
keep to the timetable.
We had ten minutes wait at the Jones farm last night, just
because hed promised to get some farm-fresh eggs for his
wife.
Itll be dark soon. Ive just remembered. Weve forgotten to get
our prescriptions at the chemists.
Were going to have to leave them till tomorrow. No, Ill run
along and fetch them while you keep the driver talking. Lets
hope he hasnt tried to be punctual for once, especially since
theyre all talking about writing to the companys complaints
department: he mightve overheard them, and I wouldnt put it
past him to give us all a nasty shock by turning up early for
once.
Whos that man with the peaked cap at the bus stop?
I expect its one of those inspectors. The busll be late tonight,
thats for sure.

2.1.4   *Add the apostrophes missing from this conversation:*

"Whereve you been? Ive been waiting three quarters of an hour."

"Im sorry were late; wedve got here sooner if it werent for the buses. Theyre worse than ever. After twenty minutes wait two came together."

"Thats all right; its not your fault. The others have gone on to queue for the tickets."

"What times it due to start?"

"Its supposed to start at eight. Wheres Sue and Chris?"

"Theyll be a bit late I expect, because Janes baby-sitting for them. Shes probably been held up at the hairdressers as usual. It doesnt matter though—theyve got tickets already, so dont worry. Chriss car is on the road again, so they shouldnt be too long; and one of Sues sisters can always look after the baby if theres any doubt about Janes getting there in time."

2.2.1   The conversations in 2.1.3 would have needed quotation marks to separate what was spoken from explanation concerning the speakers ('he said', 'she answered', etc.), if such explanation had been given.

In books, conversations are normally marked with single quotation marks ('. . .').

In handwritten accounts, double quotation marks tend to be used (". . .").

Single quotation marks are normally used when quoting single words or short phrases (see 'he said', 'she answered' above). This can be quite helpful, especially when you want to make a quote within a quotation!

"Well," Mrs Jones continued, "if you'd heard the tone of voice in which she said 'thank you, madam' you'd agree with me. She's too superior to serve ordinary folk, like you and me."

Note carefully the positions of commas, exclamation marks, question marks, and full stops in relation to the quotation marks in the following conversations. Full stops are always followed by capital letters. Commas, since they mark pauses inside sentences, are only followed by capital letters, *firstly* when the speaker's name is the next word:

"I'm cold." He shivered, wrapping his coat more tightly round him.

"I'm cold," he said, shivering and wrapping his coat more tightly round him.

"I'm cold," David said.

and *secondly* when they separate an introductory explanation from the beginning of what is said:
> David said, "It's cold outside."

> He replied, "That's why I'm staying at home tonight."

Exclamation marks and question marks are treated like commas before the words of explanation:
> "Gracious!" she exclaimed. "It's snowing! Winter's here!"
> "Why are you wearing skis?" he asked. "It's only an inch deep!"
> "But do you remember last year? We were held up for days in that blizzard," she replied.
> "But that was in Switzerland, not Birmingham!" he answered.

Note the pattern:
" ,"	"I'm cold," he said.
," ."	He said, "I'm cold."
" ?"	"Where?"
" ," ." " ."	"I'm cold," he said. "There's going to be a frost tonight."
" ," ," ."	"I'm cold," he said, "and hungry."

Remember (*see 1.1.6*) when interrupting two sentences spoken by 'he said', etc., to separate them with a full stop:
> "I'm cold," he said. "There's going to be a frost tonight."

If one sentence ("I'm cold and hungry") is interrupted, use commas:
> "I'm cold," he said, then added, "and hungry."

Add full stops or commas as appropriate where caret ($\curlywedge$) marks appear in this story:
> An old lady on a crowded train kept asking the ticket-collector to tell her when they reached Derby $\curlywedge$ the ticket-collector promised $\curlywedge$ but he was very busy $\curlywedge$ and the train had already pulled out of Derby when he remembered the old lady $\curlywedge$ he quickly told the guard $\curlywedge$ who pulled the communication cord $\curlywedge$ the engine-driver backed the train into the station again $\curlywedge$ the guard grabbed the old lady's luggage and told her to hurry up $\curlywedge$ as this was Derby $\curlywedge$ "Oh $\curlywedge$

thank you ⌄ but I'm not getting off here ⌃" she said ⌃ "you
see ⌃ I have no watch ⌄ and my daughter told me that when
we reached Derby it would be time to take my pills ⌃"

*Read the following passage out aloud, then add the necessary full stops,
question marks, commas, and apostrophes:*

George said his father was travelling with another fellow
through Wales, and one night they stopped at a little inn,
where there were some other fellows, and they joined the
other fellows, and spent the evening with them.

They had a very jolly evening and sat up late and by the time
they came to go to bed they (this was when Georges father was
a very young man) were slightly jolly too they (Georges father
and Georges fathers friend) were to sleep in the same room
but in different beds they took the candle and went up the
candle lurched up against the wall when they got into the
room and went out and they had to undress and grope into
bed in the dark this they did but instead of getting into
separate beds as they thought they were doing they both
climbed into the same one without knowing it—one getting
in with his head at the top and the other crawling in from the
opposite side of the compass and lying with his feet on the
pillow

There was silence for a moment and then Georges father
said "Joe"

"Whats the matter Tom" replied Joes voice from the other
end of the bed

"Why theres a man in my bed" said Georges father "heres
his feet on my pillow"

"Well its an extraordinary thing Tom" answered the other
"but Im blest if there isnt a man in my bed too"

"What are you going to do" asked Georges father

"Well Im going to chuck him out" replied Joe

"So am I" said Georges father valiantly

There was a brief struggle followed by two heavy bumps on
the floor and then a rather doleful voice said "I say Tom"

"Yes"

"How have you got on"

"Well to tell you the truth my mans chucked *me* out"

"Sos mine I say I dont think much of this inn do you"

"What was the name of that inn" said Harris

"The Pig and Whistle" said George "Why"

"Ah no then it isnt the same" replied Harris

"What do you mean" queried George

"Why its so curious" murmured Harris "but precisely that
very same thing happened to *my* father once at a country inn

Ive often heard him tell the tale I thought it might have been the same inn"

2.2.2 *Punctuate the following conversations:*

A woman riding along on a bus was eating peanuts. Trying to be friendly, she offered some to the woman who sat beside her.

Goodness no said the second woman Peanuts are fattening
What makes you think that asked the first
My dear exclaimed the second haven't you ever seen an elephant

Mr Smith saw a group of boys clustered round a small dog. His son Johnny was in the group.

What are you doing asked Mr Smith
Swapping lies said Johnny The chap that tells the biggest lie gets the puppy
Why when I was your age I never thought of telling lies said Mr Smith
Okay you win Mr Smith The dogs yours said one of the boys

An American was visiting Australia.

Dont you think that bridge is beautiful asked the Australian host
Well now said the American weve got bridges as big as that or bigger at home
What about this park asked the Australian Have you ever seen any like it before
Why sure said the American Weve got lots of parks bigger than that at home
They continued walking till they came to a field. Suddenly they saw a kangaroo hop by. Well said the American one thing Ill have to admit Your grasshoppers are a little larger than ours at home

2.2.3 *Punctuate the following passages, adding capital letters where necessary and starting a new line for each speaker:*

The absent-minded professor drove his car into another at a crossroads his was not damaged but the strangers car was crushed ring me up and tell me how much the repairs cost Ill pay the bill he told the stranger and started to drive away whats your number its in the telephone directory the professor called back but whats your name oh its in the telephone directory too

The absent-minded professors telephone rang in the middle of the night is that Central double-two, double-three the voice at the other end asked no this is Central 2233 the absent-minded professor replied sorry to have bothered you oh thats quite all right said the professor I had to get up anyway to answer the phone

oh dear oh dear moaned the absent-minded professor he was standing in a bus holding on to the rail with one hand while his other hand clutched a lot of bundles is there anything I can do to help you sir asked a sympathetic fellow-passenger why yes there is if you dont mind said the professor would you please hold on to this rail so that I can get my fare out

The absent-minded professor said to another professor Id hardly recognize you youve changed so much youve put on a great deal of weight and your hair has turned grey and you dont wear glasses any longer what has happened to you Professor Dixon but Im not Professor Dixon came the answer remarkable youve even changed your name

2.2.4   *Punctuate the following conversation, starting a new line when there is a change of speaker:*

the packing was done at 12.50 George said he was ready for bed we were all ready for bed Harris was to sleep with us that night and we went upstairs we tossed for beds and Harris had to sleep with me he said do you prefer the inside or the outside I said I generally preferred to sleep *inside* a bed Harris said it was old George said what time shall I wake you fellows Harris said seven I said no six because I wanted to write some letters Harris and I had a bit of a row over it but at last split the difference wake us at 6.30 George we said George made no answer and we found on going over that he had been asleep for some time so we placed the bath where he could tumble into it on getting out in the morning and went to bed ourselves it was Mrs Poppets that woke me up next morning she said do you know that its nearly nine o clock sir nine o what I cried starting up nine o clock she replied through the keyhole I thought you was a-over-sleeping yourselves I woke Harris and told him he said I thought you wanted to get up at six so I did I answered why didnt you wake me how could I wake you when you didnt wake me he retorted now we shant get on the water till after twelve I wonder you take the trouble to get up at all um i replied lucky for you that I do if I hadnt woken you youd have lain there for the whole fortnight

2.2.5

Write the conversation that you think will take place when Fred Basset's owner comes back from the hairdresser's, taking care to punctuate it correctly.

2.2.6

Write the conversation that you imagine will take place between the policeman here and the one who had to deal with Fred Basset's horn-blowing when they meet in the canteen at the police station.

2.2.7   Write a conversation that you imagine might develop from one of the following lines:

"Isn't it terrible the way . . . gossips. I've just overheard him/her saying that we should . . ."

"I hear you've just won the pools . . ."

"Tell me, headmaster, why has my son been expelled?"

"If you win the title of Miss World, what will you do?"

2.3.1   Punctuate the following:

We got to Waterloo at eleven and asked where the 11.05 started from of course nobody knew nobody at Waterloo ever does know where a train is going to start from or where a train when it does start is going to or anything about it the porter who took our things thought it would go from number two platform while another porter with whom we discussed the question had heard a rumour that it would go from number one the station-master on the other hand was convinced it would start from the local

In the paragraph above the conversation is *reported*. The author has summarized what was said when he and his friends asked three people the same question. If he had quoted the answers directly, it would have looked something like this:

"No . . . nobody at Waterloo ever does know where a train is going to start from . . ."

"I think it will go from number two platform," said the porter who took our luggage.

"I've heard a rumour that it will go from number one," said another.

"It starts from the local," the station-master assured us. "I'm certain of it."

Notice the changes that have been made to the verbs 'thought' 'had heard', 'would go', 'would start'. Why are these changes necessary?

Continue changing the conversation from reported (indirect) speech into direct speech, putting quotation-marks around the words you imagine were actually spoken at the time of the conversation.

To put an end to the matter we went upstairs and asked the traffic superintendent, and he told us that he had just met a man, who said he had seen it at number three platform. We went to number three platform, but the authorities there said that they rather thought that train was the Southampton express, or else the Windsor loop. But they were sure it wasn't the Kingston train, though why they were sure it wasn't they couldn't say. Then our porter said he thought that it must be it on the high-level platform; said he thought he knew the train. So we went to the high-level platform and saw the engine-driver, and asked him if he was going to Kingston. He said he couldn't say for certain of course, but that he rather thought he was. Anyhow, if he wasn't the 11.05 for Kingston, he said he was pretty confident he was the 9.32 for Virginia Water, or the 10 a.m. express for the Isle of Wight, or somewhere in that direction, and we should all know when we got there.

2.3.2   *For further practice in changing direct speech into reported speech, rewrite the conversations in 2.2.2/2.2.3, or those you have imagined in 2.2.5/2.2.6/2.2.7. Besides changing the tenses of verbs, be careful with words like those in bold type in these examples:*

"I am delighted to be **here**"—He/she said that she was delighted to be **there**.

"There is no prettier place at **this** time of year"—In his/her opinion there was no prettier place at **that** time of year.

"I am looking forward to staying with **you** for the **coming**

45

week"—He/she looked forward to staying with **them** during the week **that followed.**

2.3.3   *Imagine you are a reporter for a newspaper: write a longer account of one of these stories, including interviews with the people concerned. Your report of the interviews will include both direct quotation of what is said by those interviewed and also reported summaries: for example,*

When questioned about the missing jewels, the police would make no comment. The owner said that she had known nothing about the robbery until she returned from her holiday in the South of France. "It was a terrible shock," she told me. "You see, I thought I'd locked them away in the safe, but when I got back I discovered that the safe hadn't been touched."

Catastrophe

OWNERS of the Mill Hotel in Sudbury, Suffolk, which is being renovated, have ordered the return of a mummified black cat to its grave under the floorboards where it was buried by superstitious East Anglians who believed that it would ward off fire. The cat was removed four years ago by a building contractor who blames two fires and a subsiding wall on his tampering with fate.

Out-munched

OSWALD the goat, who was bought to keep the graveyard tidy at St Oswald's RC church at Ashton in Makerfield, has munched his way out of his job. After four years he has grown too fat to manoeuvre between the gravestones.

Mounting python

MR IAN ST JOHN of Kensington, London, yesterday found a five-feet-long West African royal python snake on his kitchen window ledge four storeys above street level. A snake expert from London Zoo said the snake was probably an escaped pet which had been sunning itself on the roof of the flats.

From *The Guardian*

2.3.4   *Boy* (eating an apple): Gosh! I just swallowed a worm.
Neighbour: Come into the house and I'll give you something for it.
Boy: No, thanks, I'll just let it starve.

Dialogues in plays are set out in this way, the name of the speaker printed in italics or capitals, and what is said being preceded by a colon. Any action or information on how the speech is to be said is given in brackets.

Now change the following dialogue into a conversation with quotation marks, adding any explanation you think necessary (for instance, how do you imagine the second speech to be said—defiantly? quietly? . . .). Write the explanations in the past tense:

The Chairman entered. "This this week's batch of young offenders?" he demanded, briskly, as he sat down at his desk and glanced at the pile of cases waiting for his attention . . .

CHAIRMAN: This this week's batch of young offenders?

HARRY: Yes, sir.

CHAIRMAN: Not bad this week. What did he do?

HARRY: Threw a bottle at a policeman, sir.

CHAIRMAN: It's the likes of you gets football a bad name, lad. Throwing bottles at policemen. That's not good. A policeman doesn't walk round the track to be thrown at. Do you, constable?

POLICEMAN: No, sir.

CHAIRMAN: They like to see the match and all, you know. Don't you, constable?

POLICEMAN: Yes, sir.

CHAIRMAN: They're only human, aren't you constable?

POLICEMAN: Thank you, sir.

CHAIRMAN: Well, the club won't stand for this, lad. I'm going to give you a rebuke.

HARRY: Sir.

CHAIRMAN: An official rebuke. You're officially rebuked.

HARRY: Yes, sir.

(*Enter HARRY's mother*)

MOTHER: Harry. You're in custody. I never thought I'd see the day when you'd be in custody.

CHAIRMAN: He threw a bottle. I've given him a shock, that's all. Given him a shock. Take him home and find out why he did it, will you?

MOTHER: Oh, I will, sir. I will.

CHAIRMAN: Find out why he did this, will you? All right, Harry. Go with your mother.

HARRY: Am I all right?

CHAIRMAN: This time. Go on, hurry along. Before I change my mind.

(*Exit HARRY and MOTHER*)

(Peter Terson, *Zigger Zagger*)

2.3.5 *The short story from which the following extract is taken,* The Monkey's Paw *(by W. W. Jacobs) has been adapted for the stage. Imagine you are making the adaptation. Change the presentation of the conversation into a dialogue that actors could follow easily:*

(A friend of an elderly couple has been persuaded, much against his will, to part with a lucky charm, or talisman, given to him in India. It is a monkey's paw, and whoever owns it is supposed to have three wishes granted; but previous owners have found these wishes to have ended in disaster. The first wish of the old couple has been granted: £200 has arrived, but in insurance money following the death of their only son at work, when he was caught up in a machine.)

The room was in darkness, and the sound of subdued weeping came from the window. He raised himself in bed and listened.

"Come back," he said, tenderly. "You will be cold."

"It is colder for my son," said the old woman. . . . "*The paw!*" she cried, wildly. "The monkey's paw!"

He started up in alarm. "Where? Where is it? What's the matter?"

"I want it," she said, quietly. "You've not destroyed it?"

"It's in the parlour, on the bracket," he replied, marvelling. "Why?"

"I only just thought of it," she said, hysterically. "Why didn't I think of it before? Why didn't *you* think of it?"

"Think of what?" he questioned.

"The other two wishes," she replied, rapidly. "We've only had one."

"Was that not enough?" he demanded, fiercely.

"No," she cried triumphantly; "we'll have one more. Go down and get it quickly, and wish our boy alive again."

"Good God, you are mad!" he cried, aghast.

"Get it," she panted; "get it quickly, and wish—Oh, my boy, my boy!"

"Get back to bed," he said, unsteadily. "You don't know what you are saying."

"We had the first wish granted," said the old woman, feverishly; "why not the second?"

"A coincidence," stammered the old man.

"Go and get it and wish," cried his wife, quivering with excitement.

The old man turned and regarded her, and his voice shook. "He has been dead these ten days, and besides he—I would not tell you else, but—I could only recognize him by his clothing. If he was too terrible for you to see then, how now?"

"Bring him back!" cried the old woman, and dragged him toward the door. "Do you think I fear the child I have nursed?"

2.4.1   *Add punctuation marks and capital letters to the following passage:*
he was awfully cold to be sure I half expected to see him drop down before my face and die of deadly cold his eyes looked so awfully hungry too that when I handed him the file and he laid it down on the grass it occurred to me he would have tried to eat it if he had not seen my bundle

whats in the bottle boy said he

brandy said I

he was already handing mincemeat down his throat in the most curious manner more like a man who was putting it away somewhere in a violent hurry than a man who was eating it but he left off to take some of the liquor he shivered all the while so violently that it was quite as much as he could do to keep the neck of the bottle between his teeth without biting it off

I think you have got the ague said I

Im much of your opinion boy said he

its bad about here I told him youve been lying out on the meshes and theyre dreadful aguish rheumatic too

Ill eat my breakfast afore theyre the death of me said he Id do that if I was going to be strung up to that there gallows as there is over there directly afterwards Ill beat the shivers so far *Ill* bet you

He was gobbling mincemeat meatbone bread cheese and pork pie all at once staring distrustfully while he did so at the mist all round us and often stopping even stopping his jaws to listen some real or fancied sound some clink upon the river or breathing of beast upon the marsh now gave him a start and he said suddenly

youre not a deceiving imp you brought no one with you

no sir no

nor give no one the office to follow you

no

well said he I believe you you'd be but a fierce young hound indeed if at your time of life you could help to hunt a wretched warmint hunted as near death and dunghill as this poor wretched warmint is

something clicked in his throat as if he had works in him like a clock and was going to strike and he smeared his ragged rough sleeve over his eyes

pitying his desolation and watching him as he gradually settled down upon the pie I made bold to say I am glad you enjoy it

did you speak

I said I was glad you enjoyed it

thankee my boy I do

I had often watched a large dog of ours eating his food and I now noticed a decided similarity between the dogs way of eating and the mans the man took strong sharp sudden bites just like the dog he swallowed or rather snapped up every mouthful too soon and too fast and he looked sideways here and there while he ate as if he thought there was danger in every direction of somebodys coming to take the pie away he was altogether too unsettled in his mind over it to appreciate it comfortably I thought or to have anybody to dine with him without making a chop with his jaws at the visitor in all of which particulars he was very like the dog

(Charles Dickens, *Great Expectations*, chapter 3)

2.4.2   *Add punctuation marks and capital letters to the following passage (continued from 1.4.4):*

As they drew nearer I tried to move but was powerless although I could see and hear all that went on around me two or three of the soldiers jumped from their horses and knelt beside me one of them raised my head and placed his hand over my heart

good news comrades he cried his heart still beats

then some brandy was poured down my throat it put vigour into me and I was able to open my eyes fully and look around lights and shadows were moving among the trees and I heard men call to one another they drew together uttering frightened exclamations and the lights flashed as the others came pouring out of the cemetery pell-mell like men possessed when the farther ones came close to us those who were around me asked them eagerly

well have you found him

the reply rang out hurriedly

no no come away quick quick this is no place to stay and on this of all nights

what was it was the question asked in all manner of keys the answer came variously and all indefinitely as though the men were moved by some common impulse to speak yet were restrained by some common fear from giving their thoughts

it—it—indeed gibbered one whose wits had plainly given out for the moment

a wolf—and yet not a wolf another put in shudderingly

no use trying for him without the sacred bullet a third remarked in a more ordinary manner

serve us right for coming out on this night truly we have earned our thousand marks exclaimed a fourth

there was blood on the broken marble another said after a pause the lightning never brought that there and for him is he safe look at his throat see comrades the wolf has been lying on him and keeping his blood warm

the officer looked at my throat and replied

he is all right the skin is not pierced what does it all mean we should never have found him but for the yelping of the wolf what became of it asked the man who was holding up my head and who seemed the least panic-stricken of the party for his hands were steady and without tremor

it went to its home answered the man whose long face was pallid and who actually shook with terror as he glanced around him fearfully there are graves enough there in which it may lie come comrades come quickly let us leave this cursed spot

(Bram Stoker, *Dracula's Guest*)

2.4.3 *Add punctuation marks and capital letters to the following passage (continued from 2.3.5):*

wish she cried in a strong voice
it is foolish and wicked he faltered
wish repeated his wife
he raised his hand I wish my son alive again

the talisman fell to the floor and he regarded it fearfully then he sank trembling into a chair as the old woman with burning eyes walked to the window and raised the blind

he sat until he was chilled with the cold glancing occasionally at the figure of the old woman peering through the window the candle-end which had burned below the rim of the china candlestick was throwing pulsating shadows on the ceiling and walls until with a flicker larger than the rest it expired the old man with an unspeakable sense of relief at the failure of the talisman crept back to his bed and in a minute or two afterward the old woman came silently and apathetically beside him

neither spoke but lay silently listening to the ticking of the clock a stair creaked and a squeaky mouse scurried noisily through the hall the darkness was oppressive and after lying for some time screwing up his courage he took the box of matches and striking one went downstairs for a candle

at the foot of the stairs the match went out and he paused to strike another and at the same moment a knock so quiet and stealthy as to be scarcely audible sounded on the front door

the matches fell from his hand and spilled in the passage he stood motionless his breath suspended until the knock was repeated then he turned and fled swiftly back to his room and closed the door behind him a third knock sounded through the house

whats that cried the old woman starting up
a rat said the old man in shaking tones a rat it passed me on the stairs

his wife sat up in bed listening a loud knock resounded through the house

its Herbert she screamed its Herbert

she ran to the door but her husband was before her and catching her by the arm held her tightly

what are you going to do he whispered hoarsely

its my boy its Herbert she cried struggling mechanically I forgot it was two miles away what are you holding me for let go I must open the door

for Gods sake dont let it in cried the old man trembling

youre afraid of your own son she cried struggling let me go Im coming Herbert Im coming

there was another knock and another the old woman with a sudden wrench broke free and ran from the room her husband followed to the landing and called after her appealingly as she hurried downstairs he heard the chain rattle back and the bottom bolt drawn slowly and stiffly from the socket then the old womans voice strained and panting

the bolt she cried loudly come down I cant reach it

but her husband was on his knees groping wildly on the floor in search of the paw if he could only find it before the thing outside got in a perfect fusillade of knocks reverberated through the house and he heard the scraping of a chair as his wife put it down in the passage against the door he heard the creaking of the bolt as it came slowly back and at the same moment he found the monkeys paw and frantically breathed his third and last wish

the knocking ceased suddenly although the echoes of it were still in the house he heard the chair drawn back and the door opened a cold wind rushed up the staircase and a long loud wail of disappointment and misery from his wife gave him courage to run down to her side and then to the gate beyond the street lamp flickering opposite shone on a quiet and deserted road.

(W. W. Jacobs, *The Monkey's Paw*)

3 Spelling—introductory

3.1   The assignments in the following chapters are intended as reminders of the main patterns in English spelling, and focus on approaches that should be helpful when trying to decide on the spelling of a particular word. This book cannot possibly deal with all the words that are likely to cause difficulty and is no substitute for a dictionary—but working through the assignments may help you to think about spelling in ways that will be of use to you when writing other words that do not appear here. When deciding on the spelling of a word it is important to be aware of:

the word's function in the sentence you are writing (see later in this chapter);
the way it is sounded when spoken (chapter 4);
the effect of changing the end of a word by adding another letter or group of letters (chapter 5);
the differences in spelling caused by English having absorbed elements of other languages (e.g. Latin, French, Greek), and the ways in which words and parts of words originating in other languages can be built up into longer words (chapter 6).

Most of the words chosen for the assignments have been frequently spelled incorrectly by candidates for external examinations, as is the case with the words in the assignments with which this chapter begins. Many people meet the following problems when trying to spell a word:

they are not sure of the order of two consecutive letters (e.g. **ie** or **ei**);
they are not sure whether to write a single letter or to repeat it (e.g. **c** and **s** in *occasional*);
they find that some letters do not match a word's pronunciation (e.g. *thorough*).

These difficulties are illustrated by these words: how many of them can you spell correctly? Write out each word fully, underlining the letters you insert. Each word is unfinished. Which letter is missing?

choc . late	defin . te	exist . nce
cu . board	d . scription	experi . nce

gover . ment	maint . nance	re . lize
immediat . ly	necess . ry	reco . nize
independ . nt	ple . sant	sep . rate

In these words two letters are missing: can you say which?

bel . . ve	dec . . ve	hurr . . dly
bu . . ness	ev . . ything	par . . lel
chang . . ble	fr . . nd	psy . . ology
con . . ience	fur . . us	r . . thm
continu . . s	humo . . us	su . . rised

These words can be completed by adding one letter—but sometimes it needs
to be repeated (e.g. 'di—icult = 'difficult')

acce—ible	disa—ointment	occu—ed
a—reement	di—atisfied	su—essfully
a—ount	emba—ass	to—ether
begi—ing	exa—erate	usua—y
co—espondence	ha—iness	
di—appear	occa—ional	

Each dot represents a missing letter. Decide which word is being defined, then
fill in the gaps with the letters you think are missing:

Example

ac . . m . . . . . . on   —adaptation: adjustment: obliging-
ness: an arrangement or com-
promise: space or room: lodging: a
loan of money

= accommodation

arg . . . nt   —a reason put forward in support of
an assertion or opinion: discussion,
dispute

c . . r . . ter   —a letter or distinctive mark: any
essential feature or peculiarity: a
person of remarkable individuality:
a personality as created in a play or
novel

de . . s . . n   —the act of deciding: a settlement: a
judgment

d . v . l . p   —to lay open by degrees: to bring to a
more advanced or more highly
organized state: to show, reveal the
symptoms of (e.g. a habit, a disease):
to make (a photograph) visible by
treating the film or plate with
chemicals: to grow into

int . . l . . . nt	—endowed with the faculty of reason: alert, bright, quick of mind
mis . . . lan . . . s	—mixed or mingled: consisting of several kinds
op . . rt . . . ty	—an occasion offering a possibility or chance
pos . . s . . on	—act, state, or fact of having or holding as an owner
q . . . e	—a pigtail: a line of persons waiting their turn
re . e . . t	—a written acknowledgement of anything received
r . . . . ty	—state of being responsible: what one is responsible for
s . m . . . r	—somewhat like, resembling
th . r . . . re	—for that or this reason: consequently
th . r . . . h	—complete: very exact and painstaking (of a person, his methods, or his work)
t . . . y	—agreeing with fact: correctly, accurately: properly so called, genuinely
umb	—a covered collapsible frame carried in the hand, as a screen from rain or sun: a protection, a general cover
u . . . l	—to the time when
W . . . . . d . y	—fourth day of the week
w . . . . . n	—made of, or pertaining to, wool

Check your answers by referring to this list below where the words have been arranged in alphabetical order. Underline or ring any word that caused you difficulty, and copy out its correct spelling.

accessible	changeable	deceive
accommodation	character	decision
agreement	chocolate	definite
amount	conscience	description
beginning	continuous	develop
believe	correspondence	disappear
business	cupboard	disappointment

dissatisfied	maintenance	rhythm
embarrass	miscellaneous	separate
everything	necessary	similar
exaggerate	occasional	successfully
existence	occurred	surprised
experience	opportunity	therefore
friend	parallel	thorough
furious	pleasant	together
government	possession	truly
happiness	psychology	umbrella
humorous	queue	until
hurriedly	realize	usually
immediately	receipt	Wednesday
independent	recognize	woollen
intelligent	responsibility	

The above list gives examples of only a tiny proportion of hundreds of common spelling errors. Some words—like *Wednesday, queue*—can only be learned by looking at them carefully and using them often. Although there are rules which can help us to spell efficiently, many of them have awkward exceptions which are harder to remember than the rules themselves! So it is essential that you always check your written work very carefully, and have a dictionary as a constant companion: you may find it helpful to compile your own alphabetical spelling list of words that cause you difficulty.

Look carefully at the words you have spelled incorrectly. Can you detect any patterns in your mistakes? For instance, what is common in the spelling of these groups of words? Where can mistakes easily occur?

accessible		
accommodation		
occasional	occasionally	occasional
occurred		
opportunity		
possession		
successfully	successfully	successful
	usually	usual
		until

believe	disappear	business
deceive	disappointment	furious
experience	dissatisfied	happiness
friend		
hurriedly		
receipt		

When compiling your list of words that cause you difficulty, you may find it useful to print the letters that give you trouble (e.g. diFFiculty, usefuL). *Rewrite the following words, printing the letters or groups of letters that you have found need care:*

agreement	embarrass	parallel
amount	exaggerate	realize
beginning	furious	rhythm
believe	happiness	similar
business	immediately	together
changeable	intelligent	truly
conscience	miscellaneous	until
develop	necessary	usually
disappear	occurred	woollen

3.2

When the English tongue we speak,
Why is 'break' not rhymed with 'freak'?
Will you tell me why it's true
We say 'sew' but likewise 'few'?
And the maker of the verse
Cannot cap his 'horse' with 'worse'?
'Beard' sounds not the same as 'heard';
'Cord' is different from 'word';
'Cow' is 'cow' but 'low' is 'low'
'Shoe' is never rhymed with 'foe';
Think of 'hose' and 'whose' and 'lose',
And think of 'goose' and yet of 'choose',
Think of 'comb' and 'tomb' and 'bomb';
'Doll' and 'roll' and 'home' and 'some';
And since 'pay' is rhymed with 'say',
Why not 'paid' with 'said', I pray?
We have 'blood' and 'food' and 'good',
Wherefore 'done' but 'gone' and 'lone'?
Is there any reason known?
And, in short, it seems to me
Sounds and letters disagree.

The spelling of a word may not match its pronunciation. The same letter or combination of letters may represent different sounds, as is shown in this anonymous poem. As a further example, read these words aloud, and listen for the different sounds made by the letters **ou**

bough   cough   through   tough

Another point to remember is that words may contain letters that are not sounded.

3.2.1 *Read these words aloud, then write them, printing the letters that are not sounded, or do not make the sounds that you would expect them to make—for instance, listen carefully to the sounds made by the e's in the first word:*

correspondence	government	recognize
cupboard	independent	responsibility
definite	maintenance	separate
description	opportunity	surprised
everything	receipt	thorough
existence		

So the way a word is pronounced is no key to the way it must be written (e.g. how do you pronounce the letter a in 'February' or the letter t in 'patient'?).

Re-write the following words, which have been given their phonetic spellings:

a-kros'	—from side to side of: on or to the other side of
āk	—a continued pain
bihāv-yòr	—conduct (of persons, things): manners
biz'nis	—trade, profession or occupation: one's concern or duty
kat-är'	—a discharge of fluid due to the inflammation of a mucous membrane, esp. the nose
sem'-e-tèr-i	—a burying-ground
kon'shèns	—the knowledge, or the consciousness of, our own acts and feelings as right or wrong
kres'ènt	—shaped like the new or old moon
di-sēv'	—to mislead: to cheat: to disappoint
di-zīn'	—plan in outline: preliminary sketch: pattern
e-fish'ènt	—capable of doing what may be required (e.g. of a person)
for'in	—belonging to another country, alien
frāt	—the lading or cargo, esp. of a ship
hang'kèr-chif	—a piece of material for wiping the nose, etc.
in'tri-kàt	—involved, complicated
in-trēg'	—indirect or underhand scheming or plot
ī'land	—piece of land surrounded by water
nol'-ij	—assured belief: information: familiarity gained by experience: learning
presh'us	—of great price or worth: cherished
stum'àk	—belly: place where food is digested
thûrò	—complete: painstaking (of a person, his methods, or his work): very exact and whole-hearted, or exhaustive
thöt	—the act of thinking
vej'e-tà-bl	—an organized body without sensation and

vish'us

voluntary motion, nourished by roots fixed in the ground: a plant grown for food
—having a vice or defect: depraved: malicious (e.g. remarks)

Wenz'dā
—fourth day of the week

3.2.2. *Complete these words with their missing letters:*

a . ja . ent   . . t . matic   awk . . rd   behav . . ur.

br . . k . ge   car . ful . y   cert . f . c . t .   chang . able

c . ara . ter   choc . l . te   c . mf . rt . b . .

condem . ed   contem . tu . us   cor . espond . n . e

c . usin   crit . . ize   d . . ision   defin . t .   d . scribe

el . g . n . e   emer . en . y   ev . rything   exper . . n . e

fav . . r .te   fic . . on   fr . . nd   fri . . t . ning

ind . pend . nt   h . pocr . sy   le . sure   med . . in .

li . . tning   maint . n . nce   man . . . vre

Medit . . . anean   min . . t . r .   ne . es . . ry

nons . ns .   pea . . ful   pens . .n   pe . s . . de

priv . l . ge   pro . ed . re   respons . ble   ref . r . nce

regretfu . . y   rec . . mend   reg . la . ion   rel . tiv .

rog . .   sep . r . te   seq . .nce   sil . o . et . .

str . . . ht   stren . . . en   to . ether   tra . . dy

undo . . tedly   v . . lent

3.2.3 *Use each of these words twice, in two sentences, to show that it can have two different meanings:*

file, mail, plane, race, rent, roll, scales, tip

Homophones are words which have the same sound as another, but a different meaning and origin. Example:

The children were playing on the *beach*.

Beech trees are common in Southern Britain.

Think of a homophone for each of the following words, and then use both words in sentences that will illustrate their different meanings, noting carefully the differences in spelling:

ascent   berth   board   canvas   cord   draught   gate
grater   hall   hew   manner   miner   moan   muscle
pain   pair   pale   paws   peak   pier   plum   pray   prise
rain   ring   sail   seam   seed   serial   sort   sore   some
steak   story   wait   weak   wave

3.2.4   *Complete the following sentences with one of the words in brackets:*

I   you to stay at home during this bad weather (advice, advise)

The film had a powerful   on the audience, who all decided to give up smoking (affect, effect)

The notice says that smoking is not   during the performance (aloud, allowed)

Taking the corner too fast, he tried to   and went into a skid (break, brake)

For the first   there was a choice of soup or fruit juice (coarse, course)

The   accounts are being inspected by an auditor (company's, companies)

The sash   needs repairing on that window (chord, cord)

There was a long   waiting at the bus stop (cue, queue)

The only   was his aged mother, who was bed-ridden and infirm (dependant, dependent)

For   we had treacle pudding and custard (desert, dessert)

He had to show the policeman his driving   (licence, license)

Vera Lynn did wonders for the troops'   with her songs (moral, morale)

To get to the cinema you have to drive   a church and the railway station (past, passed)

The   manager gave me a good interview, so I hope to get the job (personal, personnel)

She had to   her piano every evening for an hour (practice, practise)

The   of the college is a distinguished lawyer (principal, principle)

She bought that ridiculous hat in the January   (sail, sale)

When he looked over the edge of the cliff, he was confronted with a   drop (shear, sheer)

The bus collided with a   vehicle (stationary, stationery)

She gave the young man one of her hard ⸻ , and he
blushed and apologized (stairs, stares)

Looking at the spilt contents of her shopping bag, I grieved at
such a terrible ⸻ of good food (waist, waste)

These pairs of words are easily confused. *Write sentences of your own
to illustrate the meanings of the words you did not use to complete the sentences
above—having checked that you made the correct choices by looking up the
definitions of the words you used in a dictionary.*

*(Alternatively, you will find the reference 3.2.4 in the Checklist for all the
correct choices for the sentences above.)*

3.2.5 These words are often confused. They sound the same, or nearly the
same, and it is easy to confuse your reader by writing the wrong one.
*Check that you are able to distinguish between them by reading these examples
carefully:*

hear, here	I **hear** with my ears. It's **here** where I lost it, not there.
its, it's	The dog chased **its** tail. The weather's terrible: **it's** raining cats and dogs.
knew, new	"If you **knew** Susie like I know Susie . . ." Have you seen their **new** car?
know, no, now	**Now** I can see that you **know** there is **no** hope.
lose, loose	If you're not careful, you'll **lose** that **loose** button.
of, off	She took the lid **off** the carton **of** cream.
quiet, quite	Are you **quite** certain? They're as **quiet** as mice.
their, there, they're	**They're** over **there**, playing with **their** friends.
theirs, there's	**There's** a good film showing this week. The new postman confused us with next door. They had our letters, and we had **theirs**.
threw, through, thorough	The guerilla **threw** a grenade **through** the window, killing many people. The army is making a **thorough** search of the village.

to, too, two	It was **too** late for the **two** of us **to** go **to** the cinema.
weather, whether	We don't know **whether** the **weather** will be fine or not.
were, we're, where	**We're** sure we shall get there early this time. Last night we **were** late because we didn't know **where** to meet you.
whose, who's	**Who's** coming with us? I hope that new girl, the one **whose** brother is a professional footballer, will bring him too.
write, right	I hope you're **right** this time. Don't **write** the wrong address on the envelope again.
your, you're	**You're** going to fall over if you don't tie **your** shoelaces.

Now fill the gaps in these sentences with words chosen from those listed above.

"Those children are t . . q . . . . for my liking. Can you h . . . anything?"

"T . . .'. . playing in t . . . . bedroom. Y . .'. . worrying unnecessarily."

"You may think w .'. . lucky t . have such little angels, but this morning Susie t . . . . her milk over the cat, and Jimmy made a t . . . . mess o . the bathroom when he found y . . . can o . shaving cream. He got the cap o . . and discovered he could w . . . . with it—all over the walls and mirror."

"W . . . . w . . . you while he was decorating the bathroom?"

"In h . . . , rescuing the cat from Susie. She was trying t . pull i . . tail o . . . I can't be in t . . places at once. If you k . . . what i .'. like, staying in this house all day in this foul w . . . . . . , you'd realize why I'm suspicious n . . . ."

"All r . . . ., t . . . .'. n . need t . l . . . y . . . temper. W . . . .'s the paper? I left it over t . . . . this morning, by the television."

"The last time I saw it they w . . . looking at it. I'm not sure w . . . . . . they took it with them upstairs."

"Oh n .! I .'. probably in shreds by n . . . Listen—w . .'. crying?"

"Susie's got a l . . . . tooth. I expect Jimmy's been practising dentistry."

3.2.6   *Fill the gaps with words from the column on the left.*
(Each dot represents a letter.)

hear	"..... have you been? I .... you'd
here	never get here."
its	"It took a long time to get .... the
it's	customs. They made a .... search of all my
knew	baggage. Luckily, I ..... the gun overboard
know	when we left Calais."
lose	"I expect you had a rough crossing in this foul
loose	......."
new	"Yes, the weather is terrible. I was wondering
now	.... it would be better to delay coming
quiet	.... for a few days."
quite	"..... did you hide the money?"
right	"Why do you think I .... such large clothes?"
they're	"I wondered why your suits are usually two
their	sizes too big for you. Have you got it with you
there	...?
thorough	"Don't worry, ... safely hidden. .....
thought	looking thoughtful. What's the matter?"
threw	"It's just that I don't .... if I can trust you.
through	Where .... you on Friday?"
to	"You know very well ..... I was. I was in
too	Paris waiting for the others."
wear	"Were you really? Then why is it that ......
we're	in prison now?"
weather	"They're fools, that's why. If they had
were	managed to keep ..... in the past, they'd be
where	here with us—instead of over ..... serving
whether	time. You .... they would split on us again,
who's	given the chance, surely? They had to be kept
whose	quiet; so I .... it might be useful to .....
write	the police a helpful, anonymous letter. So ....
your	safe at last."
you're	"Are you ..... sure about this?"

"I wonder what ..... story was. We don't
know .... they've told the police
everything, or whether someone else has decided
to write a revealing letter as well."

"You're ... pessimistic. I'm usually .....
about these things, aren't I?"

"You'd better not be wrong, that's all. Their
power may be greater than you think—and ....
letter may have made problems for us as well.
Who's to say we're not being followed?"

"You worry ... much about those two kids.

.... the boss of this outfit, anyway? ..... side
are you on?"
  "Then you didn't .... the news on the
radio?"
    "What news?"
    "That ... gunmen have seized a woman in
Paris?"
    "Which woman?"
    ".... wife."

3.2.7   *Complete the following sentences with appropriate words:*
    The referee thinks you w— t— r— during football pra— .

    On his way thr— the town he pas— Mr and Mrs Brown taking
    th— dog for a walk.

    The licensee of a public house is li— to sell wines and spirits.

    He said his thoughts al— , br—ing the q— of the room.

    The arrow went o— co— , missing the target; so we —ew we
    w— going to fail the contest.

    Do you —w w— th— going to have the reception? I seem to
    have lost my invitation card. It was on the mantelpiece, but
    isn't th— any more.
    Do you l— things just when you need them?

3.3   *Function.* When you look up the spelling of a word in a dictionary
    you will notice that before the definition of the word's meaning
    there is an abbreviation of a grammatical term—n. (noun), vb.
    (verb), adj. (adjective), adv. (adverb), for instance.

3.3.1   *Noun*—a word used as a name.
    Examples—February, cigarette, community.
       *Complete the nouns in the following sentences. Each dot represents a
    missing letter. e.g. Febr . . ry. If you are in any doubt, use your dictionary to
    help you decide which letters have to be added to complete the words. These
    words are often misspelled—for the reasons given at the beginning of this
    chapter.*
       The housewi . . s were searching for barg . . ns. Their
       at . . . . . . n was drawn to various artic . . s, especially
       refri . . . . . . rs and other eq . . . . . nt for the ki . . . . . n.
       However, none of the items for sale was backed by a
       g . . r . . . .e, and so they soon lost int . . . st and joined the
       q . . . . s waiting for bu . . s, trying to hide their
       dis . . p . . . . ment by grumbling at the conduct . . s.

He was breathing without dif . . . . . . y now and his temp . . . . . e was normal. The op . r . . . . n had been a suc . . . s, and he no longer needed the as . . s . . . . e of ox . . . n. He had learned painfully the ab . r . v . . . ion for a particularly deadly p . . s . n.

The pr . . . . . . l of the col . . . e suddenly remembered his eng . . . ment; he checked the advert . . . ment in his newsp . . er and discovered that the evening p . . form . . . . started in twenty min . . . s. Fearing he was going to be too late to gain admi . . . . n, he drove as fast as he dared. On this oc . . . ion he was lucky, apart from a near col . . . ion with a stud . . . riding a b . . . . le, and reached the th . . t . . without being stopped by a police of . . . er. His driving li . . . . e had been endorsed twice already, once during the previous for . . . . . t. Unfortunately, his return j . . . . . y ended in di . . s . er: he had forgotten that his fuel g . . . e was not working, and so had to walk several kilom . . . . s to the nearest filling st . . . . n in a remote vil . . . e.

Write the correct spellings of these nouns, which have been written phonetically as in a dictionary to indicate their pronunciation:

kampān'	—the time during which an army keeps the field: organized action in support of a cause
kar'ij	—a vehicle for carrying
kas'e-rōl	—a stew-pan: a vessel in which food is both cooked and served: the food itself (Fr.)
kas-et'	—a holder with reel of magnetic tape, esp. tape on which there is pre-recorded material (Fr.)
kat'a-log	—a classified list of names, books, etc.
kat'e-gor-i	—what may be affirmed of a class: a class or order
kol'i-flowr	—a variety of cabbage
sel'ar	—any underground room or vault, esp. where stores are kept
sen'tū-ri	—any sequence of a hundred
sèr-tif'i-kát	—a written declaration of some fact
chan'l	—a navigable passage: means of communication
sur'kum-stans	—a fact or event, esp. in relation to others
shed'ūl (U.S. sked'-ūl)	—a time-table, plan, programme or scheme
siz'órz	—a cutting instrument with two blades

3.3.2   *Verb*—a word used to express an action, thought or feeling.
Examples—believe, develop, exaggerate, occur.
(Complete the spelling of the following verbs (see instructions for 3.3.1).

ag . . .   —to get on with one another: to consent: to
                    concur (with)

ap . l . . . . e   —to make excuse: to express regret for a fault

at . . m . t   —to try or endeavour: to try to do

op . r . . e   —to work: to work (e.g. a machine): (surg.) to
                    perform some unusual act upon the body
                    with the hand or an instrument

p . r . . . ve   —to become or to be aware of through the
                    senses: to see: to understand: to discern

pr . . t . . e   —to put into practice: to perform: to do
                    habitually: to exercise oneself in any art
                    (esp. music)

pr . . . . e   —to go before in time, rank, or importance

pro . . . d   —to go on: to continue (with): to take legal
                    action

re . . . ze   —to feel strongly, or comprehend completely:
                    to bring into being or fact, to accomplish,
                    achieve: to make real, or as if real

re . . . ve   —to take, get, or catch, usu. more or less
                    passively: to have given or delivered to one:
                    to admit, take in, or serve as receptacle of:
                    to meet or welcome on entrance: to give
                    audience to, or acknowledge socially: to be
                    acted upon by, and transform electrical
                    signals

r . p . . t   —to say, do, or perform again: to quote from
                    memory: to recount: to divulge: to say or
                    do after another

s . . ze   —to take possession of suddenly, eagerly, or
                    forcibly: to snatch or grasp: to take prisoner

s . . . .st   —to put into one's mind: to imply or seem to
                    imply: to propose: to hint (to)

y . . . d   —to resign: to grant: to give out, to produce

*Write the correct spelling of these verbs, which have been written
phonetically as in a dictionary to indicate their pronunciation:*

ak-sept'   —to take (something offered): to receive
                    (e.g. one's fate) without demur: to take
                    upon oneself (e.g. a task, responsibility: to
                    receive with approval or favour, as
                    adequate or true: to agree to pay

a-kum'pan-i   —to go with: to attend, escort: to
                    supplement (with something)

66

a-dres′	—to speak or write (to) (also noun: a speech; the place to which a letter is directed: a place of residence)
a-nowns′	—to give public notice of: to make known
a-prē′shi-āt	—to estimate justly: to esteem highly: to raise the price of
sel′e-brāt	—to make famous: to honour with solemn ceremonies
kol-ab′or-at	—to work in association
kom-ens′	—to begin: to originate
di-zīn	—to draw: to form a plan of: to contrive: to intend, destine (also noun: a preliminary sketch, plan in outline: intention: relation of parts to the whole: pattern)
dis-kus′	—to examine in detail, or by argument: to debate

3.3.3   Check your answers to 3.3.1 and 3.3.2 with the Checklist on pp. 137–70. You may have *thought* you could spell these words correctly, but been mistaken: if so, add these words to your own list of words needing special care, printing the letters that you need to get right in future.

Occasionally the same word can be used in different ways. The function of the word *design*, for instance, could be that of a verb:

"What do you do to earn a living?" she asked.

"I *design* houses," the architect replied.

Here is the same word being used as a noun:

The committee congratulated the architect on the skilful *design* of the housing estate.

Make up sentences to illustrate how these words can be used as nouns or verbs:

address, campaign, attempt, repeat, yield

The word *repeat* could also be used in a third way:

After applauding the singer for several minutes, the audience was rewarded with a *repeat* performance of three of the songs in her programme.

Here its function is that of an adjective *(see 3.3.6 below)*. Similarly, the word *cassette* included in the list of nouns in 3.3.1 could be used as an adjective—a *cassette* recorder—giving added information about a particular type of tape recorder. (Can you think of an example of the word *design* being used as an adjective?)

These terms (noun, verb, adjective) can be useful when referring to the way a word is being used in a sentence. Occasionally you will find that it is useful to know what they mean when you have to choose between two similar spellings—as you may have found already in answering 3.2.4.:

> I   you to stay at home during this bad weather (advice, advise)

> She had to   her piano every evening for an hour (practice, practise)

A verb is intended in both of these sentences, and so the correct choice would be advise in the first and practise in the second. In this sentence, though, a noun is needed:

> He had to show the policeman his driving   (licence, license),

so the correct choice would be licence. Note the pattern:

noun	verb
advice	advise
licence	license
practice	practise

3.3.4   Care is needed when adding -ed or -ing to a verb. These endings sometimes affect the letter that comes immediately before them. For instance, note what happens to the final letter in these verbs when -ing is added to them:

kneel	steal	kill	develop
kneeling	stealing	killing	developing—*no change*

patrol	refer	—*doubled*
patrolling	referring	

deceive	rumble	
deceiving	rumbling—*dropped*	

Complete the gaps in the following lists, checking your answers with the checklist as before:

hop	hopped	ho . . ing	hope	hoped	. . . . . .
run	ran	ru . . ing	dine	. . . . .	dining
hit	hit	hi . . ing	shine	shone	. . . .
stop	. . . .	. . . .	believe	. . . .	believing
			receive	. . . .	
			notice	noticed	. . . .
			handle	. . . .	
			convince	. . . .	. . . .

(4.1.2; 4.1.4; 4.4.7)

apply	. . . .	applying	annoy	a . . o . . .	annoying
carry	carried	. . . .	destroy	destroyed	. . . .
marry	. . . .	marrying	develop	. . . .	. . . .
hurry	. . . .	. . . .			
control	controlled	controlling	call	. . . . . .	calling
fulfil	. . . .	. . . .	kiss	kissed	. . . .
travel	. . . .	. . . .	discuss	. . . .	. . . .
			possess	possessed	. . . .
prefer	. . . .	preferring	equip	. . . .	. . . .
transfer	transferred	. . . .	omit	. . . .	. . . .
occur	. . . .	. . . .			(4.4.6)

When you have checked your spellings with the checklist on pp. 137–70, look carefully at the ways in which these verbs have been grouped. Can you see the patterns in their spelling? Look at each group of verbs and say how their spelling is affected by adding -ed and -ing. For instance, in the first group the last letter in the verb is doubled before these additions (the term for additions to the ends of words that affect their function is *suffix*—see chapter 5)—run, running; stop, stopped. What happens in the second group (hope, dine, etc.)? Why should there be this difference? (If you do not know, see 4.1.4. The assignments referred to in brackets after the other groups may help you decide on the reasons for the pattern in their spellings, too).

3·3·5   *Referring to your completed (and, if necessary, corrected) lists in 3.3.4, complete the following sentences with the appropriate verbs:*

Everton's captain has been t . . . . to Leeds United. Leeds are now c . . . . that they will win the Cup next season, b . . . . that with this player they are e . . . . with the means of overcoming all opposition. Everton are h . . . . to find a suitable replacement, and the manager is t . . . . to London, where it is thought that another transfer will be d . . . .

The Government is c . . . . . . on all farmers to help in c . . . . fresh outbreaks of foot and mouth disease which have caused hundreds of cattle to be d . . . . recently.

They said that they h . . . . to get m . . . . . . in the next few weeks, and that their friends would be r . . . . invitations shortly. They p . . . . not to d . . . . . . their reasons for the delay, except that although he had a . . . . . . for several jobs, several difficulties had d . . . . Happily they had r . . . . . . news of a vacancy that would be o . . . . next week; so they thought that nothing would be s . . . . them from m . . . . soon.

Complete the gaps in the following sentences with the appropriate form of the verbs given in brackets. Some of the verbs may not appear in the lists you completed in 3.3.4, but the patterns illustrated in those lists may help you to decide how to spell verbs when adding -**ed** or -**ing**:

(Run) to catch the train, she nearly (trip) over a small boy who was (hop) from one side of the platform to the other. In her haste she had (pass) the ticket barrier without (notice) the ticket collector, who, not (believe) that she (possess) a ticket, (call) her back to him, (stop) her from (get) on the train. While searching through her handbag for the ticket, she suddenly remembered her two suitcases, and (hurry) back to the ticket office, where she thought she had left them. Bitterly she remembered the long walk up the hill from the bus stop, (carry) two heavy cases, several carrier bags—she had been (shop) on the way—and an umbrella: now she (regret) not having (travel) in a taxi! Her luggage had gone: worse still, she had (omit) to check that it had been (label) correctly. She was not (surprise) to see the train (leave) the platform on her return from the lost property office.

(Dispute) the management's decision, the union wanted to explore other possibilities. (Compare) the foreman's conduct with that of other employees, the management thought their complaints were (exaggerate), and (decide) to replace him with a trainee, (believe) that this would settle the dispute. (Fascinate) by the advertisement, and (prefer) a job demanding some responsibility, she (apply) for the vacancy and was successful. On her first day she was (accompany) by the manager, who (introduce) her to her new colleagues. Although at first a little (embarrass), and often (confuse) their names, she (persevere) and was soon (satisfy) that in (choose) to leave her previous job she had made the wisest decision of her career.

3.3.6   *Adjective*—a word added to a noun to qualify it, or to limit it by reference to quality, number, or position.
Examples—A *worried* man, a *poor* harvest, *forty* thieves, the *nearest* villa.

Adverb—a word added to a verb, adjective or other adverb to express some modification of the meaning or an accompanying circumstance.

Examples—He arrived *safely*, and *soon* found out what had happened. He was *very* excited, laughing and joking *very loudly*—*too loudly* for my ears.

Complete the adjectives and adverbs in the following passage (see instructions for 3.3.1).

The old ladies found a help . . . friend in their new neighbour. He was bas . . . . ly an affect . . . . . . person, and although im . . n . . ly strong, was c . . . te . . s, gent . . and pa . . . . t. His help was al . . . s av . . . . b . . and he freq . . . . ly did h . . v . man . . . jobs for them about the house and in the garden, working q . . . kly, car . . . . ly and ef . . . . . ntly. He was partic . . . . ly skil . . . with anything requiring a mec . . . . . . l knowledge, having, before his retirement, prev . . . . ly worked in electrical engineering. As they grew older they became ent . . . ly depend . nt on him. They were tr . ly gr . . . f . ., and felt their thanks were insuf . . . . . nt, but, a sens . t . . . and ind . pend . . t person, he would never accept their contin . . . offers of payment. Every fortnight they would invar . . . ly invite him to a spe . . . l tea: he would arrive pr . . . tly at four o' clock, us . . . ly bringing with him flowers or vegetables from his garden.

Give the correct spellings of the following adjectives and adverbs:

b . . . . . . ble   —that may be believed
ben . f l   —useful, advantageous
compar . t . . . ly   —estimated by comparing with something else: not positive or absolute
compar . b . .   —that may be compared (with): worthy to be compared (to)
def . . . . nt   —wanting, lacking
del . b . . . . .   —intentional; considering carefully: cautious
del . . . t .   —pleasing to the senses, esp. the taste: dainty: frail, not robust: refined in manners: polite, considerate
del . . . . . s   —highly pleasing to the senses, esp. taste: affording exquisite pleasure
dif . . . . nt   —distinct, separate: unlike, not the same
ef . . . . . v .   —having power to produce a specified effect: powerful; striking (e.g. illustration, speech)
ex . . . . . nt   —surpassing others in some good quality: of great virtue, worth, etc.
ext . . . ive   —large, comprehensive

hid . . . s	—frightful, ghastly, horrible: extremely ugly
imp . r . . nt	—of great weight, significance, or consequence
inf . n . t .	—without end or limit
in l	—commencing: of, at, or serving as the beginning
l . . . e	—slack: unbound: free: indefinite, vague: unrestrained
mis	—prone to mischief
pers . . . . nt	—constantly recurring or continued (e.g. efforts)
p . . s . n . . s	—having the quality of destroying life or impairing health
prim . . . ly	—originally: chiefly
rad . . . . ly	—thoroughly: bent on drastic but constitutional reform
re . . . . ly	—relatively near in past time
r	—straight, direct: true, genuine
r . t . . n	—decaying: corrupt: unsound: disintegrating

3.3.7   Adverbs are often formed by adding the suffix -**ly** to an adjective (e.g. particular, particularly). Sometimes care is needed with the letters that come before this suffix (just as when adding -ed or -ing to a verb). For instance, when adding -**ly** to careful, make sure that both ls are written—*carefully*.

Change the following adjectives into adverbs:

beautiful	definite	clumsy
helpful	entire	easy
successful	fortunate	necessary
occasional	immediate	satisfactory
original	inadequate	
principal	precise	
special	reasonable	
	safe	
	scarce	
	separate	
	sincere	
	true	

As before, check your answers with the Checklist on pp. 137–70.

Note the pattern: usual + ly   = usually
hopeful + ly   = hopefully
rare + ly   = rarely

There is no change in the spelling of the word from which the adverb has been formed: there are two ls in *hopefully* because the word has been formed by adding -ly to the adjective *hopeful*. Similarly, the e at the end of nearly all the adjectives in the second column remains when these words are changed into adverbs. Why are *reasonably* and *truly* exceptions to this pattern, do you think? How would you spell adverbs formed from *responsible, agreeable, appreciable, terrible*?

What is the pattern when adding -ly to the adjectives in the third column? Does it remind you of a similar pattern in one of the groups of verbs listed in 3.3.4?

3.3.8   *Fill the gaps in the following sentences with adjectives or adverbs taken from the list you have made in 3.3.7:*

"At the third stroke, it will be four fourteen . . . . ly"

A hospital spokesman said he was making s . . . . progress.

The concert was s . . . . The e . . . . . audience rose to its feet, cheering and whistling. The fans p . . . . wanted to hear the final number again, and would shout all night if n . . . . F . . . . they didn't have to wait long. At the first chord they were i . . . . silent.

He d . . . . wanted to come with us, but only o . . . . left work before six. He was r . . . . certain that he wouldn't be late, but if he was delayed we were to go s . . . ., as he could e . . . . . catch us up.

3.3.9   *Complete the pattern in the list below:*

Noun	Adjective	Adverb
joy	joyful	
peace		
beauty		
care		
	happy	
	sincere	
	real	
necessity		
privacy		
quiet		
safety		
satisfaction		
success		hopefully

The complete groups of words are included in the Checklist. In each case the spelling of a word has been changed to show a different function by altering its ending: the word *happy* is used as an adjective

> The happy children

and is changed into an adverb by adding **-ly**

> The children played happily

and into a noun by adding **-ness**

> As we watched the children laugh and play, their happiness was obvious.

Make up sentences to show how the spelling of other groups of words in this list is changed according to their function.

3.4   *Recap.* The assignments in chapter 5, *Suffixes*, look in more detail at the spelling of the ends of words, where changes in spelling show a difference in *function* rather than in meaning: (e.g. satis**fact**ion—noun, satisfa**ctory**—adjective, satisfactori**ly**—adverb (*see 3.3.9*). The assignments in chapter 6, *Roots and Prefixes*, concentrate on the spelling of the beginnings of words, where, in contrast, changes show a difference in *meaning* (e.g. **un**satisfactory means the opposite of satisfactory); this chapter may also help to explain why English spellings have so many inconsistencies!

All the words whose spellings you have completed in this chapter are frequently mis-spelled by candidates in examinations. If, on checking your answers with the Checklist on pp. 137–70 you have found that you have made any mistakes, try to avoid them in future by

1 compiling a list of the words that give you difficulty, printing the letters that need care;
2 keeping this list by you to refer to when you write;
3 when writing other words whose spelling is unfamiliar to you, look them up in your dictionary.

You may have difficulty in spelling some words that appear for the first time in later assignments, or do not appear in this book: if so, add them to your list. It may be, though, that these words correspond to some of the patterns noted in these assignments, and understanding these patterns may be all that is required. For instance, when changing the form of a verb ending in -y to show a past tense (time), you had to change its spelling not only by adding -**ed**, but also by changing the **y** to **i**:

> carry, carried.

Similarly, in changing adjectives ending in -y to adverbs by adding -**ly the y** was changed to **i**:

> clumsy, clumsily.

You will also have noticed that when adding -**ed** (and -**ing**) to some verbs, sometimes the final letter in the verb was doubled and sometimes not.

hope, hoped
hop, hopped
develop, developing
equip, equipping

While always remembering the point made in 3.2.1 above, that the spelling of a word does not necessarily match its pronunciation, there are some patterns in spelling caused by the ways in which words are pronounced—the sounds made when they are spoken. The assignments in chapter 4 will remind you of some of these patterns, and understanding these patterns will help you to distinguish the spelling of *hoped* from *hopped*, *developing* from *equipping*—and also help you to approach the spelling of other words not necessarily included in the assignments of this book.

4 Spelling—sounds

There are some patterns in spelling caused by the ways in which words are pronounced when spoken. The assignments in this chapter will remind you of some of these patterns.

4.1.1 Long/short vowels

Complete the following lists:

cry	cried	crying	have	having
fry	. . . .	frying	come	. . . . .
spy	. . . .	. . . . . .	shine	. . . . . .
try	. . . .	. . . . . .	smoke	. . . . . .
worry	worried	. . . .	hope	. . . . .
carry	. . . . . .	carrying	write	. . . . . .
marry	. . . .	. . . .	notice	. . . .
hurry	. . . . . .	. . . .	stare	. . . . . .
			decide	. . . .

What are the spelling patterns in these lists? Complete these sentences:

Verbs ending in -y change . . . . before adding -ed, e.g.
. . . .   *(Check with the Recap section 3.4)*

When adding -ing to verbs ending in e . . . .,
e.g. . . . .

Now read each pair of words aloud. How does the spelling affect the way you say the words?

shine	shin
dine	begin
hope	hop
smoke	smock
clothe	cloth
moment	comment
elope	develop
opening	occurring

(See 4.1.2 below)

Read the following words aloud, also listening for the differences in sound made by the vowel letters a e i o u:

hid	head	had	bud	hod	hood	sitter
heed	fool	hard	hoard	heard		

Each of the vowel letters a e i o u has two sounds—
a long vowel sound hate   here   hide   hope   tube
(i.e. imitating its alphabetical name)

and a short vowel hat   her   hid   hop   tub
sound

In some words the vowel sounds are written with two vowel letters—
rain   straight   seed   boat
Say whether the vowels in bold type are long or short:

angel	float	reign
angle	head	said
any	height	sign
aisle	island	soldier
baby	knife	solemn
comb	listen	stupid
empty	mend	tune
female	open	ugly
feminine	mop	weight
find	pancake	wrinkle

Dictionaries often show the difference between long and short vowel sounds by a - over a long vowel sound
āngel   cōmb   tūbe
and a ˘ over a short vowel sound
ăngle   mŏp   ŭgly
Add the appropriate symbol to the vowel letters printed in bold type in these words:

battery   bungalow   crochet   crossing   glacier   magistrate
miscellaneous   necessity   knee   prehistoric   puny
social   recuperate   tornado   vacuum

4.1.2   *Complete the following tables with further examples:*

Usual spellings for long vowel sounds

long vowel	Initial		Medial		Final	
(ā)	a	apex	a-e	cape	ay	say
	. . . . .				. . . . .	
	. . . . .				. . . . .	
	. . . . .				. . . . .	
	. . . . .				. . . . .	

(ē)	e	equal	ee	feet		ee	bee
				. . . . .			. . . . .
				. . . . .			. . . . .
				. . . . .			. . . . .
			e-e	athlete (2 syllables)*			
				. . . . .			

(ī)	i	icon	i-e	five		y	fly
				. . . . .			. . . . .
				. . . . .			. . . . .
				. . . . .			. . . . .
						ie	pie
							. . . . .

(ō)	o	open	o-e	hope		ow	glow
				. . . . .			. . . . .
				. . . . .		o	potato
				. . . . .			. . . . .

(ū)	u	unit	u-e	tube		ue	statue
							. . . . .
						ew	few
							. . . . .

* *syllable*—this term is explained in 4.4 below.

Notice the *medial* pattern in this list, the

a—e
i—e
o—e
u—e

pattern, where the e is not sounded when the word is spoken, but indicates that the previous vowel is a long one:

tāle tīre tōne tūbe

This 'silent' e helps us to distinguish

shīne	from	shĭn
dīne	from	dĭn
hōpe	from	hŏp
clōthe	from	clŏth

The 'silent' e usually remains when adding suffixes that begin with consonant letters. (4.1.1. referred to the *vowel* letters a e i o u: all other letters are called *consonants*.)

hope hopeful hopefully hopefulness hopeless
hopelessly hopelessness time timely timeless

but is omitted when adding a suffix with a vowel, like -ed and -ing. There are not two es in *hoped* or *timed*, and similarly the 'silent' e does not appear when writing (write + ing = writing) *hoping* or *timing*. (Think about the confusion that could occur if the e did remain.)

Look back at the list of verbs ending in e in 4.1.1, and note the pattern there (*have* looks like an exception to this pattern: if you look up 4.3.9 you will see another reason for the e at the end of this word). *What is the pattern in the spelling of the verbs in the list below?*

hop	hopped	hopping
stop	stopped	stopping
shop	shopped	shopping
drag	dragged	dragging
control	controlled	controlling

With verbs ending in a consonant letter, the usual pattern is for this letter to be repeated before adding a suffix:

hop + p + ed = hopped

drag + g + ing = dragging

This is always the case for words of one syllable, like *hop, stop, drag*, and is often the case with verbs of more than one syllable, like con-trol, controlling, be-gin beginning; but it is not so with some verbs—for instance o-pen opening, de-vel-op, developing.

There is another pattern working here, and this is explained in 4.4.6.

A repeated consonant letter, then, indicates that the vowel letter before it has a short vowel sound. If you were learning English as a foreign language, this spelling pattern would help you in pronouncing these words:

diner	dinner
later	latter
super	supper
planing	planning
writing	written

Similarly, being aware of the ways in which these words are pronounced will help you to spell them correctly, and to avoid confusing them in your writing. When deciding whether to write a consonant letter once or to repeat it, it may be helpful to think of the sound made by the vowel letter before it: if it is a short sound, usually the consonant letter that follows will be repeated, and if it is a long sound it will be followed by a single consonant:

mōment	cŏmment
written	wrīting

A consonant is doubled only when there is one consonant sound after a short vowel sound: if there is more than one consonant after a short vowel sound no doubling takes place—mended (not menndded).

Add -ing to the following verbs, adapting their spelling where necessary:

ache	greet	keep	make	spoil	speak	take	write	pipe
call	grit	kick	mask	spill	spit	tell	wait	strip
change	shield	tempt	tune	tug	urge	view	win	stick

Diphthong—two vowels brought together, their sounds blending into one syllable (*see 4.1.3*) e.g. oi, oy, ou, ow.

Complete this table as in 4.1.2:

(au, aw)	*au*	August	*au*	haul	*aw*	paw
		. . . . .		. . . . .		. . . . .
				. . . . .		. . . . .

(ai)	*ai*	ail	*ai*	faint		
				. . . . .		
				. . . . .		
				. . . . .		
				. . . . .		

(oi, oy)	*oi*	oil	*oi*	boil	*oy*	boy
				. . . . .		. . . . .
				. . . . .		. . . . .
				. . . . .		. . . . .
				. . . . .		. . . . .

(ou, ow)	*ou*	out	*ou*	stout	*ow*	now
	ow	owl		. . . . .		. . . . .
				. . . . .		. . . . .
			ow	gown		. . . . .
				. . . . .		. . . . .
				. . . . .		

To recap, you should now be able to see why the verbs at the end of the assignment 4.1.2 could be grouped like this:

ache	aching	greet	greeting	call	calling
change	changing	keep	keeping	spill	spilling
make	making	shield	shielding	tell	telling
pipe	piping	speak	speaking		
take	taking	spoil	spoiling	grit	gritting
tune	tuning	view	viewing	spit	spitting
write	writing	wait	waiting	strip	stripping
				tug	tugging
urge	urging	kick	kicking		
change	changing	mask	masking		
		stick	sticking		
		tempt	tempting		

All the verbs in the first group have a long vowel sound indicated by a silent **e**, which is removed when adding the suffix -**ing**. *Change* changes to *changing* for a second reason, linking it with *urge urging*: here the **e** is used for another purpose—*urge*, like *merge*, *verge*, *purge*, *surge*—does *not* have a long vowel sound, but the **e** that follows the **g** in each of these verbs softens the sound made by the letter **g** when they are spoken. This point is developed further in *5.1.1 (and see 4.3.2 below)*.

No doubling of consonant letters takes place in the verbs listed in the second column, since *greet* and *keep* are examples of verbs that end with a consonant letter that follows a *long* vowel sound, the same sound being made by two vowel letters in the verbs *speak* and *shield* (*see 4.4.6 below*); *spoil, view*, and *wait* have diphthong sounds made by two vowel letters, and the same pattern applies when adding -**ing** as occurs with long vowel sounds; *kick, mask, stick* and *tempt* are examples of verbs with short vowel sounds followed by two consonant letters.

The first group of verbs in the third column also end with two consonant letters, in this case the same letter repeated (can you think of any word in English with three **l**s in succession?). Only the final group of verbs illustrates the pattern formed by adding -**ing** to a verb ending with a single consonant letter that follows a short vowel sound.

All these verbs are words of one syllable—before adding -**ing** to them. The patterns for verbs of more than one syllable are dealt with in 4.4.6 below.

If you have had any difficulty with these assignments, make sure you learn these patterns:

1 Double the final consonant of *one-syllable* words with *one short vowel* followed by *one consonant* before a suffix beginning with a vowel, e.g.

    shop + ing = shopping
    shop + er = shopper
Exceptions (see 4.3.9)
    give—giving
    have—having
    live—living
    love—loving, etc.

These verbs have short vowels—but no word in English ends in -**v**, and the same pattern applies here as with:

2 Drop the final **e** of silent e words before a suffix beginning with a vowel, e.g. hate + ing = hating.

Exceptions
    dye + ing = dyeing
    singe + ing = singeing

```
acre  + age = acreage
mile  + age = mileage
free  + ed  = freed
free  + er  = freer
```
These words keep their silent e—despite the addition of a suffix beginning with a vowel—to make sure that their meaning remains clear. For instance, *freed* would otherwise be confused with *Fred*! Make up sentences of your own to show the difference in meaning between

singing and *singeing*
dyeing and *dying*

3 Keep the final e of silent e words when adding a suffix beginning with a consonant, e.g. hate + ful = hateful.

Exceptions
```
argue  + ment = argument
awe    + ful  = awful
due    + ly   = duly
nine   + th   = ninth
true   + ly   = truly
true   + th   = truth
whole  + ly   = wholly
```
If any of these exceptions (and those in 1 and 2 above) were unfamiliar, add them to your list of words needing special care. You may find this mnemonic helpful, too: fill the gaps in this sentence:

Tru—, Mr Du—, your nin— argu— is whol— aw—, and that's the tru—.

(See also 4.4.7, 5.1.1, 5.1.2)

4.2.1   **ie or ei?**
Read these words aloud:
        ceiling   deceive   field   fiend   receive
What is the pattern for the order of i and e when making the long vowel sound ee?
Complete the following words with **ie** *or* **ei***:*
        bel . . ve   misch . . vous   conc . . ve   ch . . fly
        bur . . d   p . . ce   p . . rce   perc . . ve
        ach . . vement   conc . . ted

                                            (Answers in 4.5.7)

Note carefully the exceptions to this pattern:
        Write *i* before *e*
        Except after *c*
        Or when sounded like *tray*
        As in n**ei**ghbour and w**ei**gh

And except *seize* and *seizure*
And also *leisure*
Weird height and *either*
Forfeit and neither

With the exceptions of *seize* and *weird*, the i before e except after c when the sound is ee jingle is worth remembering!

In the other examples above, a different sound is indicated, as is the case here:

ancient audience foreign heiress (and heir—e.g. to the throne, as distinguished from the hair on the heir's head) society (read this word aloud—*so-ci-e-ty*—and think of associated words, like social) sovereign (like foreign). and counterfeit (sometimes pronounced like forfeit).

Complete the following sentences:

We were dec— into bel— the misch—vous boys. N—ther of them returned, having s—zed our bur—d treasure after we had spent hours digging in the f—ld without rec—ing any reward. The w—rd sh—ld p—rced with holes once containing precious stones was to have been the prize possession of the Soc—ty for Anc—nt Archaeology, but now was —ther lost or sold to another unsuspecting victim.

Would you like a p . . ce of apple p . . ?

The h . . ress had to forf . . t a large amount of her fortune to pay the ransom to the kidnappers, who had s . . zed her cousin.

He always buys for . . gn cars.

Can you guess my h . . ght and w . . ght?

How do you spend your l . . sure time?

The pr . . st said he would keep his sermon br . . f.

Our n . . ghbours have complained to the landlord about the state of their c . . lings.

The aud . . nce bel . . ved the dec . . ts of the conjurer.

In anc . . nt times many cities suffered s . . ges during war.

The maniac conc . . ved the w . . rd idea that he was ruler of the world.

4.2.2.   **e or ee?**
          Complete the gaps in these sentences with e or ee:
          If you proc—d at this rate, you will succ—d in exc—ding the
          sp—d limit.

          The pr—c—ding bad weather was followed by sunshine.

          'Interc—d— ' means 'to plead on behalf of', 'act as a
          peacemaker between two' and 'supers—d—' means 'to
          replace', 'render unnecessary'—what does 'ant—c—d—nt'
          mean?

          Check your answers with the lists on pp. 137–70, and make sure
          you do the same with your answers to the assignments that follow.

4.2.3   **y or ey?**
          *Complete the gaps in the following sentences with **ey** or **y**:*
          He went on a journ— to a beautiful vall— near the
          boundar— between Hampshire and Surr—, where the fields
          were sown with wheat and barl—.

          After assembl— we have to go to the librar—.

          I feel wear— today; I don't seem to have the abilit— to find
          an— energ— for an—thing involving activit—.

          He was robbed of all his mon—y when walking through a
          dark all—.

          They were hoisting the heav— replacement stone onto the
          abb— roof by means of a pull—.

          Among his favourite sports are hock— and voll—ball.

          He hoped his pet monk— had not tried to climb up the
          chimn—.

          Are you read— for your steak and kidn— pie, or would you
          prefer some cold turk— sandwiches?

          I eat my peas with hon—
          I've done so all my life;
          It makes the peas taste funn—
          But it keeps them on the knife.

          The letters **ey** make the vowel sound ($\bar{a}$) in some words, e.g. they.
          *Which words ending in -**ey** would fit the following definitions?*
          to carry: to transmit: to impart, communicate: to make over
          in law

84

to render obedience: to submit

booty, plunder: an animal that is, or may be killed and eaten by another: a victim

to provide, furnish, supply

to see or look over: to take a general view of: to inspect, examine: to measure and estimate the position, extent, and contours of (e.g. a piece of land)

4.2.4   **e or ea?**
Most of the words in which ĕ is spelled **ea** are short, common words connected with everyday-life (examples: elephant, head). Unfortunately, there are as many short words spelled with **e**! Therefore, when in doubt, you must check with your dictionary before choosing which spelling to use. *Complete the gaps in the following sentences:*
We had to tr . . . carefully, spr . . . ing out and keeping in a st . . . y rank, thr . . . ing our way through the long grass of the m . . . . w, each of us filled with dr . . . at the thought of stumbling on a d . . . body. Our br . . . . came out in short gasps, and the sw . . . trickled down our necks. Finding the w . . . . ns . . rl . . r m . . nt that we had the clue we had been s . . . . . ing for; but in . . . . . of feeling relieved, we knew the victims must be in h . . v . n by now, that the gang had d . . . t their revenge—and they might be lying in wait for us a . . . d. This journey was going to be far from pl . . . . nt. Our h . . . s throbbed, and we longed for a break for br . . . and cheese washed down by a pint of beer.

4.3   The assignments in this section will remind you of some common spelling patterns in words of one syllable:

4.3.1   f, l, s, z sounds are usually doubled after a short vowel (in one syllable words), e.g. buzz. *Add further examples to illustrate this pattern:*
stiff   . . . .
bell   . . . .
boss   . . . .
Complete the following sentences with exceptions *to this pattern:*
He told —s to get off the —s when it reached the —works. We did th— , and when we reached the football ground found the score was still two–n—. The cost of admission p— our fares came to one pound each.

4.3.2   g keeps its hard sound before **i** or **e** by adding a **u**, e.g. guide. *Complete the gaps in the following sentences with* gue/gui/ge/gi *as appropriate:*

They're chan—ng their minds: their verdict is likely to be 'not —lty'.

I can only —ss at the answer to your question, though I think I understand the —st of your argument.

He may be a —nius, but he is not very well organized!

She is a very affectionate person, and is —ntle and —nerous.

There is no —arantee that if she is bought a —tar she will learn how to play it, however —nuine her intentions may be.

Our —sts decided to surprise us by dis—sing themselves as Dracula and Frankenstein.

4.3.3   The **j** sound at the end of a one-syllable word containing a short vowel is spelled **-dge**. *Complete the following sentences:*

The car swerved and narrowly missed the e . . . of the bri . . .

However much one boxer tried to d . . . . round his opponent, the other refused to b . . . .

The gipsy knocked at the lo . . . door, trying to c . . . . some money or food

There was an exciting old movie showing, called 'The Red B . . . . of Courage'

She looked in the f . . . . . for some ice cubes.

4.3.4   The **k** sound at the end of a one-syllable word containing a short vowel is usually spelled **-ck**. *Give words ending in* -ck *that will fit the following definitions:*

the hinder part of the body in man, and the upper part in beasts;

of the darkest colour;

a platform extending from one side of a vessel to the other, thereby joining them together and forming both a floor and a covering;

to pass the tongue over;

a device to fasten doors, etc.;

fortune, good or bad;

to strike a blow or blows with something hard or heavy;

a large outstanding natural mass of stone;

a large bag of coarse cloth material for holding grain, flour, etc.

How is the **k** sound spelled at the end of a one-syllable word containing a short vowel, when the preceding sound is **ng**, e.g. ban— (a place where money or other valuable material is deposited)? *Give three more examples.*
How is the **k** sound spelled at the end of a one-syllable word containing a *long* vowel? *(see 4.1.4) Give three examples.*

(See also 4.4.4)

4.3.5 The **ch** sound at the end of a one-syllable word containing a short vowel is usually spelled **tch**—but there are exceptions. *Fill the gaps in the following sentences with words ending with tch or ch, as appropriate:*

They were making so m— noise that their neighbour went to f— a policeman.

He had a p— over one eye, and his face was covered with bl—es from a like of drinking nothing but rum.

The umpires inspected the p—, w— was waterlogged.

The garage told him that he would soon have to buy a new cl— for his car.

If only we were r—, we would have s— fun.

4.3.6 **q** is always followed by **u** and at least one other vowel. *Complete these words:*

q	—the cry of a duck
q	—pleasantly odd or strange, esp. because old-fashioned
q	—to tremble, esp. with cold or fear
q	—an amount that can be counted or measured
q	—a dispute: a breach of friendship
q	—an excavation from which stone is taken, by cutting, blasting, etc.
q	—a fourth part
q	—a set of four
q	—to crush, subdue
q . . .	—a wharf for the loading or unloading of vessels: a landing place
q	—an enquiry

q . . . .   —a line of persons awaiting their turn
q . . . .   —speedy: nimble
q . . . .   —at rest, calm: silent: undisturbed
q . . . .   —completely, exactly

4.3.7   **igh**, **ough**, and **augh** are usually followed by **t**. *Complete the following sentences:*
We o . . . t to have escaped, but unluckily we were c . . . . t. We m . . . t have had better luck if Jimmy hadn't been so f . . . . tened, which made us all nervous and fr . . . . t. Our prison sentences have t . . . . t us a lesson. We were b . . . . . t to justice for trying to steal what we o . . . t to have b . . . . t. None of us ever th . . . . t it would turn out like this—but we f . . . . t like madmen before they got us into this dr . . . . ty cell.

4.3.8   *Complete the following list:*
After **w** the sound o is usually spelled **a**, e.g. was.

w . . . . r	—to ramble with no definite object
w . . p	—a winged insect with biting mouth parts, slender waist and sting
w	—to look with attention
w . . . . t	—a bag for carrying necessaries: a pocket book
w . . . . w .	—to roll about in mud, etc., as an animal (implying enjoyment)
w . . . . . r	—a veteran soldier: a fighting man
w . . . . . g	—the act of cleansing by water

After **w** the sound ĕr is usually spelled **o**, e.g. work, word.

w . . . d	—the earth and its inhabitants
w	—bad or evil in a greater degree: not so well as before
w . . . . . p	—religious service: fervent esteem: adoration paid to God
w . . . . s	—of no value, virtue, excellence

4.3.9   No word in English ends in **v** or **j**. Whether the vowel is long or short the ending is **ve**. *Fill the gaps in the following sentences:*
We h . . . received f . . . pounds reward for rescuing the dog trapped in the dangerous c . . . at high tide. We intend to use the money to buy some new gl . . . s for Sue, who would l . . . to have a present on her birthday. She l . . .s alone, and nobody seems to visit her, not even her neighbour in

the flat a . . . . . She isn't well, either: last time we saw her she looked more dead than a . . . . . It will be good to g . . . her a present.

4.4 *Syllable*, sil'a-bl, n.—a word or part of a word uttered by a single effort of the voice.

Examples: you're, too, rough, through, off, course, knew, were know, where, they're, there, lose. These all have one syllable.

practice, licensed, aloud, breaking, and quiet—have two syllables.

4.4.1 *Read the following words aloud to yourself, slowly and deliberately, then write the number of syllables as a figure in brackets after each word:*

film	fortunate	immediate	impatiently
invent	modern	straight	systematically
umbrella	unnecessarily		

Write these words divided into their separate syllables, using hyphens to mark the breaks (e.g. separate syllables = sep-a-rate syll-a-bles)

ancient	brilliant	cheerful	cheerfully	difficult
disappointment	exaggerate	experience		
furious	government	immediately	maintenance	
miscellaneous	necessary	occasional		
opportunity	realize	responsibility		
successfully	usually			

The syllables of the following words have been mixed up: sort them out into their correct order:

rate-cel-e-ac	comm-date-ac-o	cum-ac-late-u
cle-cy-bi	as-cat-tro-phe	u-cur-lum-ric
el-ment-op-dev	ic-ient-eff-in	ment-rass-em-bar
ry-ru-Feb-a	ti-den-i-fy	ter-er-pret-in	i-in-on-op
ra-y-tor-lab-o	cel-mis-lan-ous-e	chol-gy-psy-o

4.4.2 Accented syllables are marked thus ', e.g. ban'dit, as-ton'ish-ing. Some of the following words are accented on the first syllable (like **ban'**dit) and others on the second (like aston'ishing). *Re-write these words, adding a ' immediately after the syllable you stress when you read the word aloud:*

asleep	broken	complete	deceive	dreaming
forget	lightning	mountain	proceed	silence

Do the same with these words of three syllables:

disappear	disappoint	festival	forgetful
galloping	innocent	interrupt	reluctant
remembrance	reunite		

4.4.3   **all** and **well** followed by another syllable only have one **l**, e.g. also. *Complete these sentences:*
"You are a— very w—come," she said. "I hope you're w—. The others are here a— dy, and Mrs. Brown hopes to come a—o, a— h she has the w— re officer with her at the moment."
(See also 5.2.3)

4.4.4   In a two-syllable word the sound **k** is spelled **ck** between two short vowels, e.g. cricket.
At the end of an unaccented syllable the sound **k** is spelled **c**, e.g. frantic.
In words of more than one syllable, the sound **k** before a consonant is spelled **c**, e.g. picnic.
Complete the following sentences with c, ck, *or* k, *as appropriate:*
As the clo— stru— ten, she pi—ed up her cloa—, ma—ing sure she —ept a tight hold of her lu—y charm, which she concealed in her po—et. She ra—ed the ashes and po—ed out the —oals in her fire and watched the smo—e —url up the chimney. Her newly-washed smo— was airing over a chair. She pa—ed a parcel of fruit and ca—e, took the plugs out of the ele—tri— so—ets, moved the bu—et out of her way, and went out, —losing the door behind her, feeling slightly wi—ed to be out at this time of night. —arefully, she pi—ed her way through the thi—ets and passed the hens who were —lu—ing softly to themselves. She li—ed her lips as she thought of the delicious jo—e she was playing, loo—ing forward to her brother's rea—tion to her tri—ing him. She imagined him searching franti—ally through the house.

4.4.5   The sound **sh** is most frequently spelled **ti, ci** and **si** at the beginning of all syllables except the first. *Complete the following words:*

an—ient	admis—on	divi—on	gra—ous
finan—al	impa—ent	man—on	musi—an
infec—ous	pala—al	na—onal	pas—onate
spa—ous	tena—ous	opera—on	permis—on
ini—al	spe—al	espe—ally	

4.4.6 *Read these words aloud, then write them, adding the ' mark immediately after the syllable you stressed when reading the word aloud:*

open   gallop   develop   control   begin   visit

Now re-write these verbs, adding the suffix -ing: is any alteration needed to their spelling? In 4.1.4 the point is made that in verbs of one syllable (like *hop, run, drag*) containing a short vowel sound and ending in a single consonant letter, this final letter is doubled before the suffix:

hopping   running   dragging

With verbs of more than one syllable, if the last syllable is accented (e.g. e-quip', con-trol', ad-mit') and ends with a single consonant preceded by a vowel (equip, control, admit) double the consonant before a suffix beginning with a vowel: equip, equipped, equipping; control, controlled, controlling; admit, admitted, admitting (similarly, the noun form admission):

Therefore you should have written:

opening   galloping   developing   controlling
beginning   visiting

The first three words are *not* accented on the last syllable when spoken:

o'-pen   gal'-lop   de-vel'-op

so the doubling does not occur, and the same is true of vis'-it.

Be careful therefore with these words: re-fer'—refer, referred, referring; but: ref'-e-rence, where the accented syllable has changed; and similarly: confer', conferred, conferring, *but* con' ference.

Do not confuse the single syllable **fit, fitted, fitting** with ben'-e-fit, benefited, benefiting.

Also, note that no doubling occurs if:

1 a suffix beginning with a consonant (e.g.-ment) is added to the root word: equipment, controls;

2 the last syllable of the root word does *not* end with a single consonant (e.g. a-ppoint', appointment);

3 the consonant is preceded by a vowel produced by two letters (e.g. a-ppear, appearance).

(*See also 5.1.5.*)

Finally, note the different pattern with verbs ending in -l, which always have this final consonant doubled before adding a suffix beginning with a vowel, whether the first or second syllable is accented:

can'cel, cancelled, cancelling, cancellation
patrol', patrolled, patrolling
e'qual, equalled, equalling
appal', appalled, appalling

Note 3 above still applies:
appeal, appealed, appealing
repeal, repealed, repealing

Complete the gaps in the following sentences:
The crime was commit— between two and three a.m.

The accident occur— outside a hospital.

The generosity of the public is greatly appreciat—.

The performance will be commenc— in three minutes.

Through the bushes I glimps— a deer.

I asked my employer for a refer—, as I was applying for a new job.

We all benefit— from the change of scene, returning refreshed and relaxed.

The manager is away at the moment, attend— a confer—.

The new laboratory is fully equip—, being fit— with the complete range of electrical equip—.

After admis— to the hospital, her case was refer— to the house surgeon.

Rather than continue quarrel— with his neighbour, he prefer— to move house, even though this would mean travel— further to and from work.

The newspapers have been cancel— while they are away on holiday.

The pupils were expel— from the school for attempt— to set fire to the library.

The cost of the materials equal— the previous month's expenditure.

(See also 5.1.4)

4.4.7   *Complete the following lists:*

travel		travelling	traveller
cancel		cancelling	cancellation
compel	compelled		compulsion
expel		expelling	expulsion
quarrel			——
equal		equalling	equation

Note the difference in the next group of verbs, where -le may sound the same as -el, but their spelling agrees with the pattern of other verbs ending in e:

tackle		tackling
tremble	trembled	
wriggle		wriggling
trifle	trifled	trifling
trouble		
grumble	grumbled	
stumble		
handle		
cease	ceased	ceasing
choose		
cleanse	cleansed	
collapse	collapsed	
commence		
condense		condensing
complete		
corrode		
contrive		
deceive		
receive		

Complete the following sentences:

The professor declare— that the declin— population would lead to a decreas— need for schools and hospitals.

The student was told that she deserv— high marks for describ— the scene so accurately.

He was determin— that despite the discourag— knowledge that his officers disapprov— of his plan he would not be deterred from discharg— his duty.

In disguis— themselves as merchants, the outlaws hoped they would be successful in entic— the soldiers into the open, thus enabl— them to win an easy victory.

While explain— the cause of the failure of the journey, he showed pictures of the fascinat— wild life they glimps— when explor— the jungle.

In making the deci— he was inspir— by the example of his uncle, whose work was gaining increas— admiration.

We were introdu— to the oppos— team, who soon pers— us that our constant pract— had been worthwhile.

Promis— us that we would not be recogn—, the captain led us out of the fort.

After its rough handl—, the horse was trembl— and kept stumbl—

4.5 Recap

4.5.1 Change final **y** to **i** when adding final suffixes *except* when the suffix begins with **i** or when **y** has a vowel in front of it, e.g.

try	tried	trying		
rely	relied	relying	reliable	reliably
play	played	playing	player	
pity	pitied	pitying	pitiful	
			pitiless	

(4.1.1. See also 5.2.2)

4.5.2 Drop the final **e** of silent e words before a suffix beginning with a vowel, e.g. hope, hoping; later = lat + er

(4.1.2–4.1.4)

but not before a suffix beginning with a consonant, e.g. hopeless, hopeful. *(See 4.5.4)*

A few words lose their final **e** when a *consonant* suffix is added *(see list in 4.1.4)*.

A few words retain their silent **e**, despite a vowel suffix being added, to keep their meaning clear *(also listed in 4.1.4)*.

4.5.3 Double the final consonant of *one-syllable* words with *one short vowel* followed by *one consonant* before a suffix beginning with a *vowel*, e.g. tap, tapping (distinguishing this verb from tape, taping—*see 4.5.2*).

Exceptions: giving, having, living, loving, etc. *(see 4.3.9)* and fix, box, mix—**x** never doubles in English.

When a vowel comes before a double consonant, it is almost always short, e.g. diner, dinner   later, latter   super, supper.

Silent **e** at the end of a word usually makes the preceding vowel long, e.g. cake, home, compose.

(4.1.2–4.1.4)

4.5.4 Add suffixes beginning with a consonant, without altering the spelling of the preceding root word, e.g. hopeful, hatless, sadly, rarely. The exception to this pattern is referred to in 4.5.1 above, e.g. playful *but pitiful*

(4.4.6)

4.5.5 Double the final syllable in two- or three-syllable words, if the final syllable is stressed, e.g. confer', conferring—*but* con'ference; begin', beginning—*but* vis'it, visited, visiting, ben'efit, benefited.

(4.4.6)

4.5.6 Words ending in **-el** or **-al** double **l** before a suffix regardless of accent, e.g. quarrel, quarrelled   signal, signalling   metallic.

(4.4.7)

4.5.7 **ei/ie** believe, mischievous, chiefly, buried, piece, pierce, achievement, *but* conceive conceited.

    -ceed, -sede, -cede:
      three **-ceed** words—succeed, exceed, proceed;
      one **-sede**—supersede;
      all others **-cede**—e.g. intercede, antecede, precede.

(4.2.2)

Not many words in frequent usage end in **ey**. Use this list to check your answers to 4.2.3 and add any words that need special care to your own list:

abbey	attorney	barley	chimney	covey
hockey	honey	jockey	journey	kidney
money	monkey	motley	parsley	pulley
Surrey	trolley	turkey	volley	

ey make the **a** sound in the following words:
    convey   obey   prey   purvey   survey   they

e spelled **ea**: *the most often used words.* Use this list to check your answers to 4.2.4 and add any words that need special care to your own list:

bread	breadth	breast	breath	dead
deaf	dealt	death	dread	head	health
heaven	heavy	lead	meadow	meant
measure	pleasant	read	ready	realm
spread	stead	steady	sweat	thread
threat	tread	treadle	wealth	weapon

Can you distinguish between the following pairs of words? Make up sentences to show their differences in meaning:
    breath, breathe; lead (sounded lēd), lead (sounded lĕd); lead (sounded lĕd), led; read (sounded rēd), read; stead, steed; sweat, sweet.

95

4.5.8 **Patterns in 4.3**

Use these lists to check your answers to these assignments. The f, s, l, z sounds are usually doubled when spelled at the end of one-syllable words after one short vowel.

stiff	cliff	sniff	but exceptions—bus	us	has
bell	tell	well	gas	of	his
boss	loss	toss	plus	nil	pal

To keep the hard sound for g, follow it with a u when spelling g before i or e: guilty, guess, guests—also guarantee.

When g is followed by i, e, or y it is sounded j. Otherwise it is sounded g as in gold: gentle, giant, gymnastics, gymnasium, generous, gist, genius, gallon, gold, guide, glass, grow.

(*Exceptions:* begin, get, girl, give, gear, geese, gift, girth, geyser, giddy.)

The j sound at the end of a one-syllable word after one short vowel is spelled dge, e.g. badge, edge, bridge, fudge, lodge, dodge, budge, cadge, fridge.   (*4.3.2, 4.3.3*)

(*See also 5.1.1*)

The k sound at the end of a one-syllable word after one short vowel is nearly always spelled ck: back, black, deck, lick, lock, luck, knock, rock, sack.

k between two short vowels in a two-syllable word is spelled ck as in cricket, bucket, etc.

k at the end of an unaccented (unstressed) syllable is spelled c—e.g. frantic, arsenic—and in words of more than one syllable it is also spelled c before a consonant, e.g. picnic, hectic.

(Other spellings of this sound, e.g. antique, quay, chemistry are derived from other languages—see Chapter 6   (*4.3.4*)

The ch sound at the end of a one-syllable word after one short vowel is nearly always spelled tch, e.g. fetch, patch, blotch, pitch, clutch. Exceptions: such, much, rich, which.   (*4.3.5*)

q is nearly always followed by u and at least one other vowel: quack, quaint, quantity, quake, quarrel, quarry, quarter, quartet, quay, quash, question (also query), queue, quick, quiet, quite.

(*4.3.6*)

igh, ough and augh are usually followed by t, e.g.: ought, caught, might, fright, fraught, taught, brought, ought, bought, thought, fought, draught.   (*4.3.7*)

ŏ after w is usually spelled a, e.g.: wander, wasp, watch, wallet, wallow, warrior, washing, was.

ĕr after w is usually spelled o, e.g. work, word, world, worse, worship, worthless.   (*4.3.8*)

No word in English ends in v, always in ve, whether the vowel is long or short, e.g. have, five, cave, cove, glove(s), love, live(s), above, alive, give.   (4.3.9)

4.5.9   Patterns in 4.4.3–4.4.5:
all and well followed by another syllable only have one l, e.g. welcome, already, also, although, welfare, always, alone.   (4.4.3)
Answers to 4.4.4—*see 4.3.4 above for explanation:*

clock	struck	picked	cloak	making
kept	lucky	pocket	raked	poked	coals
smoke	curl	smock	packed	cake
electric	sockets	bucket	closing	wicked
carefully	picked	thickets	clucking	licked
joke	looking	reaction	tricking	frantically

When c is followed by e, i, or y it is sounded s. Otherwise it is sounded k, e.g. centre, ceiling, circle, cycle, cave, cream, cottage, clever, curious.

ti, ci and si are three spellings most frequently used to indicate sh sound at the beginning of all syllables except the first, e.g.: ancient, admission, division, gracious, financial, impatient, mansion, musician, infectious, palatial, national, passionate, spacious, tenacious, operation, permission, initial, special, especially.
                                                                              (4.4.5)

4.6   **Revision**
Complete the words in the following assignments, each dot representing a missing letter. The words have appeared before in assignments in this chapter or in chapter 1, and illustrate the patterns shown in these assignments, their exceptions, and words needing special care because their spelling does not match their pronunciation.

Check your answers with the alphabetical list of spellings in the Checklist on pp. 137–70. If you have difficulty in spelling any of these words, add them to your own list of words, printing the letters that need special care.

4.6.1   *Complete the gaps in the words listed below with* **ei** *or* **ie**:

aud . . nce	n . . ghbour
bel . . ved	sc . . nce
c . . ling	soc . . ty
conven . . nt	sold . . r
dec . . ve	v . . wing
f . . ld	w . . ght
h . . ght	w . . rd
misch . . vous	

Complete the gaps in these words with one or more vowel letters:

appr . . ch	mater . . l
chang . . ble	miscellan . . . s
chimn . y	opin . . n
compl . t . ly	q . . . t
cont . . ning	soc . . l
dis . . se	sp . . king
disg . . sing	vac . . m
hid . . . s	w . . ting

fr . . ndship	l . . sure
g . . sts	m . . sured
h . . lthy	q . . stions
h . . vy	r . . d . ly

accur . t .	ident . c . l
activ . ty	incred . ble
appropr . . t .	irr . sist . ble
arb . trate	irr . tat .
b . rthday	mag . strate
b . . ght	man . g . r
dang . r . . s	marr . . ge
def . n . t .	nat . r . l
fem . n . n .	pres . nt
f . . rth	relig . . . s
fright . n . d	sent . nce
gar . ge	s . m . thing
g . . r . ntee	

Complete the gaps in these words with one or more consonant letters:

bri . . t	i . land
cau . . t	ki . king
drau . . ty	. no . ked
em . ty	lis . en
ex . use	mis . ellaneous
fas . en	res . uing
fid . et	solem .
for . ni . . t	su . . rise
fri . . ten	. riting

Complete the gaps in these words with either a single or repeated consonant letter:

a—ident	bo—ower
a—roach	ca—ing
a—ro—riate	co—ent
a—ention	cro—ing

deve—o—ing   na—owly
fina—y   o—u—ing
fo—ow   o—ening
ho—efu—   o—inion
ina—urate   o—onent
into—erable   pa—enger
i—esi—tible   su—e—fu—y
ma—ying   usua—y
misce—aneous   wo—ied

How do you spell the 's' or 'sh' sound in the gaps in these words?

arbitra . . on	nego . . ate
de . iding	pre . . ous
e . actly	pre . . ure
ex . ept	. . ien . e
ex . iting	senten . e
finan . .al	silen . e
inten . . ons	so . . al
interna . . onal	u . . ally
ne . e . . ary	

4.6.2

The king had dif . . . . lty in contro . . ing his ministers. They weren't as f . . thf . . as they ap . . . red. They were a . ways asking him for favours, tr . ing to get pardons for the . . fr . . nds, and at the sam . tim . re . . .y ho . .ng that the . . r . q . . sts would be refus᛫ . ., so they mi . .t have an op . . . t . n . ty or kil . . ng him. They were espe . . . . .y glad when he did not at . . m . t to con . e . l his anger as he us . . . . y did. The day ar . . v . d when they could put their plans into ac . . . n: one of them had been a . r . st . d for st . . l . ng the q . . . n's ne . kl . . . . Each of them de . ided that this was the mo . . nt for them to put their . ampa . . n into op . ra . . . n. They hur . . ed to the court, c . r . fu . . y hid . . g their s . ords ben . . th their clo . . s. The bri . . t sunshi . . incr . . s . d their hap . . . . . s. Soon the . . would be o . . as . .n for rej . . .ing. With the king su . . es . . u . .y o . po . . d, they could live saf . . y ag . . n. The revolution was be . i . . ing.

4.6.3

a . . ent	—act, or way of climbing or mounting up
b . . rd	—a broad and thin strip of timber: meals and lodging
bo . . d	—wearied, lacking interest
dr . . . . t	—a current of air

99

mus . . .	—an animal tissue by contraction of which movement is effected
r	—uneven: crude: coarse in texture: unrefined
ser . . .	—forming a series
af . . ct	—to make a show or pretence of
. f . . ct	—to produce, accomplish (also n.—the result, consequence, outcome)
br . . .	—to sever forcibly: to shatter: to interrupt (e.g. silence): to cure (of a habit)
br . k .	—a contrivance for retarding the motion of a wheel by friction
c . . rse	—a common, rough, or inferior
c . . rse	—path in which anything moves: the direction pursued: method of procedure
q	—a line of persons awaiting their turn
al . . . . d	—permitted: granted
al . . d	—not in a whisper or undertone, not silently
de . . rt	—a barren place
prin	—highest in rank, importance: chief
sta . . . . . ry	—standing, not moving: fixed: permanently located
was . .	—desolate: lying unused: rejected, discarded, useless

4.6.4

fortun . . .	—happening by good fortune: lucky
im	—without delay: next, nearest: direct
imp	—lacking patience
stra	—not curved or bent: direct
umb . . . . a	—a covered collapsible frame carried in the hand, as a screen from the rain or sun
ne . . . . . ry	—requiring to be done: unavoidable or inevitable
an . . . nt	—very old
bril . . . nt	—sparkling: splendid: talented
ch . . rf . .	—in good spirits: lively
dif . . . . . t	—not easy: hard to be done
dis . . p . . . tment	—the defeat of one's hopes
e . . . g . r . . .	—to magnify unduly: to represent too strongly
exp	—long and varied observation: any event

	or course of events by which one is affected
f . . . . . s	—full of fury
g . v . . . ment	—a ruling or managing: control
m . . nt . n	—the act of maintaining
mis . . . . . n	—mixed or mingled: consisting of several kinds
o . . . s . . n . .	—occurring infrequently, irregularly, now and then
op . . . tun . . .	—a possibility or chance offered by a circumstance or combination of circumstances
re . li . .	—to accomplish, achieve: to feel strongly, or to comprehend completely
r . spons . b	—state of being answerable for, deserving the blame or credit for: what one is answerable for . . .
su . . . . . f . .	—having, achieving the desired end or effect
us . . . . y	—most frequently
a . . . . . rate	—to increase the speed of
a . . . . . . date	—to furnish or supply with: to oblige: to lodge
a . . . . . late	—to heap or pile up, to amass
b	—bike
cat	—a calamity
dev . . . . ment	—a gradual unfolding or growth
embar . . . . ment	—perplexity
Feb . . . . y	—second month in the year
int . . pre . . .	—a translator
lab	—place where scientific experiments are systematically carried on
ps . . . . y	—the science that investigates the phenomena of mental and emotional life
a	—from side to side of
a . . .	—a continued pain
b . . . ness	—trade, profession or occupation: one's concern or duty
cons	—the state of realizing our own acts and feelings as right or wrong
d . . . . ve	—to mislead: to cheat
fr . . . . t	—the lading or cargo, esp. of a ship
th	—complete: painstaking
th . . . . t	—the act of thinking
vi	—having a vice or defect: depraved: malicious

We . . . . day	—fourth day of the week
car	—heedful
chan	—inconstant: fickle
cor	—relation of part to part: communication by letters
d . . . . ion	—a settlement: a judgment
d . . . rib .	—to give an account of
em	—an unexpected occurrence or situation demanding immediate action
p . . s . . d .	—to convince
priv	—an advantage enjoyed by an individual or a few
ref	—the act of referring: a testimonial
reg	—a rule prescribed esp. in the interests of order or discipline
rel	—corresponding: comparative: one who is related by blood or marriage
stren	—to make strong or stronger
t . . . . . er	—gathered to one place: in the same place, time or company

5   Spelling—suffixes

5.1   A *suffix* is a letter, or a group of letters, added to a word to change the way we use it. As has been shown in chapter 4, no spelling change is needed if the suffix begins with a consonant, if the root word ends in two consonants or in two vowels followed by one consonant: e.g. hope-less, black-ness, look-ing.

Thus the **s** in *bus* is not a suffix, but is in *trains*, showing the plural form of *train*. Similarly, the suffix **es** is added to bus to show the plural form of this word—*buses*, as also occurs with *box, boxes*. -**ing** is not a suffix in the word *ring*, but is in the word *ringing* (=is/was doing); again, -**ed** is not a suffix in *red*, but is in *bored* (=past tense: the silent **e** of *bore* has been dropped). Several assignments in chapters 3 and 4 were concerned with spelling changes caused to verbs by adding the suffixes -**ed** and -**ing** (see 3.3.4; 4.1.4. 4.4.6–4.4.7), for instance in *giving* the suffix -**ing** requires the dropping of silent **e**, as is the case in *hoping*, while a short vowel sound is indicated by a doubled consonant letter before the suffix -**ing** in *hopping*, and a stress on the second (accented) syllable is indicated in *controll'ing* by a similar doubling of the consonant letter at the end of the verb *control*. Also, in 3.3.7 it was pointed out that the suffix -**ly** turns an adjective into an adverb, occasionally affecting the spelling of the root word—*loud loudly, happy happily*; similarly, other suffixes will show that a word is being used as a noun (e.g. happi**ness**).

affect, affect**ed**, affect**ing** (verb)   affect**ion** (noun)
affect**ionate** (adjective)   affect**ionately** (adverb)
hope, hop**ed**, hop**ing** (verb)   hope**ful** (adjective)
hope**fully** (adverb)   hope**fulness** (noun)   hope**less** (adjective)   hope**lessly** (adverb)   hope**lessness** (noun)

It was also pointed out in chapter 3 that words without suffixes added can sometimes be used in different ways (*see 3.3.3*)—*hope* could be a verb (I *hope* the train isn't late) or a noun (as Christmas approached, her *hope* that her husband would be coming home grew stronger). A suffix will show the way in which a word is to be used, and understanding the form and meaning of suffixes can help you when choosing between two words that sound alike (*see 3.2.4–6*), for instance mist (noun) missed (verb).

> The hills were shrouded in heavy *mist*.
> We were late, and *missed* the last bus.

(Similarly *pact*—noun—and *packed*—verb: make up sentences to show the distinction between these two words.) The spelling of a suffix never changes, but the spelling of the word to which it is added sometimes does. The assignments in this chapter will remind you of some of these changes, and also help you to distinguish between similar suffixes (e.g. **ar/er/ure/or, able/ible**).

5.1.1   Many verbs, like disapprove and conclude, end in a silent e. When adding a suffix that begins with a vowel, omit this letter: disapprove + **ing** or **al** = disapprov(ing)(al). (*See also 4.1.2*)

Complete the following lists:

believe	believing	believable
argue	. . . .	. . . .
accept	. . . .	. . . .
excite	. . . .	. . . .
imagine	. . . .	. . . .
allow	. . . .	. . . .
recognize	. . . .	. . . .

Note the exceptions to this pattern:

> ageing   mileage   rateable   dyeing (from the word 'dye'—to stain, give a new colour to—to distinguish it from 'dying'—losing life)

change	changing	*but* changeable	—because the letters c and g are usually hard when they come before the vowels a, o and u (e.g. musical, apricot, cushion regard, gospel, figure) so the e is retained to preserve the soft sound made when c and g come before e (e.g. surgeon) i (e.g. regiment) and y (e.g. cycle)
notice	noticing	noticeable	
service	servicing	serviceable	
manage	managing	manageable	

*Each of the following words has a letter missing. Think of the sound made
by the letter before the gap when the word is pronounced. If it is a soft c or
g then add e or i: if hard add k or u:*

courag . ous	panic . ed	veng . ance	peac . able
catalog . e	vag . e	chang . able	outrag . ous
dung . on	grac . ous	fatig . e	spac . ous
intrig . e	picnic . ed	pig . on	serg . ant
mimic . ing	pronounc . able	gorg . ous	dialog . e

5.1.2   **-ing/-ion/ive**
Complete the following lists:

verb		noun
act	ac**ting**	action
affect		
collect		
consider		
discuss		
express		
inform		
object		
suggest		
associate	associated	association
celebrate		
complete		
confuse		
congregate		
describe		
emigrate		
examine		
exaggerate		
fascinate		
hesitate		
illustrate		
imitate		
prepare		
ventilate		

		adjective	noun
conclude	conclu**ding**	conclusive	conclusion
exclude			
include			
persuade			*(See also 4.4.7)*

5.1.3 -ed

Give the past tense of these verbs (e.g. suggest=suggested) *by adding the suffix* ed, *altering the spelling of the verb where necessary:*

hope	accompany	omit	satisfy	create
threaten	hop	veil	interfere	separate
persuade	persevere	compel	try	accomplish
pray	beg	acknowledge	argue	surrender
disappoint	acquire	perceive	force	clean
struggle	visit	notice	(*See also 4.1.4, 4.4.6, 4.4.7*)	

5.1.4 -ed/-ing: verbs ending in l

When adding these suffixes to verbs ending in -l, double the l if it is preceded by a single vowel, e.g. propel, propelled, propelling, but not if it is preceded by a pair of vowels, e.g. fail, failed, failing.

Complete the following list:

appeal	appealed	appealing
conceal	. . . .	. . . .
cool	. . . . . .	. . . . . .
expel	. . . .	. . . .
feel	felt	. . . .
foul	. . . . . .	. . . . . .
fulfil	. . . .	. . . .
initial	. . . .	. . . .
label	. . . .	. . . .
marvel	. . . .	. . . .
patrol	. . . .	. . . .
pedal	. . . .	. . . .
prevail	. . . .	. . . .
quarrel	. . . .	. . . .
reveal	. . . .	. . . .
shovel	. . . .	. . . .
signal	. . . .	. . . .
toil	. . . . . .	. . . . . .
total	. . . .	. . . .
uncoil	. . . .	. . . .
unveil	. . . .	. . . .
wheel	. . . . . .	. . . . (*See also 4.4.6*)

5.1.5 -ed/-ing: verbs ending in r/t

When adding these suffixes to verbs ending in -r or -t of *one* syllable, double the r or t if it is preceded by a single vowel (i.e. short vowel sound—*see 4.1.2*), e.g. jar, jarred, jarring; rot, rotted, rotting; but not if it is preceded by a double vowel or long vowel-sound, e.g. float, floated, floating; hear, heard, hearing.

When verbs of more than one syllable, if the accent is on the first syllable when the word is pronounced do not double the r or t (e.g. **brack**et, bracketed): only do so when the accent falls on the *second* syllable (*see 4.4.6*)—if the r or t is preceded by a single vowel (e.g. ad**mit**, admitted).

Complete the following lists:

air	aired	airing
alter	. . . .	. . . .
bear	(bore)	. . . .
blur	. . . .	. . . .
chair	. . . .	. . . .
cheer	. . . .	. . . .
conquer	. . . .	. . . .
defer	. . . .	. . . .
despair	. . . .	. . . .
deter	. . . .	. . . .
differ	. . . .	. . . .
enter	. . . .	. . . .
fear	. . . . . .	. . . .
filter	. . . .	. . . .
incur	. . . .	. . . .
labour	. . . .	. . . .
moor	. . . . . .	. . . .
occur	. . . .	. . . .
offer	. . . .	. . . .
order	. . . .	. . . .
pair	. . . . . .	. . . .
pilfer	. . . .	. . . .
prefer	. . . .	. . . .
recur	. . . .	. . . .
refer	. . . .	. . . .
render	. . . .	. . . .
star	. . . .	. . . .
stir	. . . .	. . . .
suffer	. . . .	. . . .
tar	. . . . . .	. . . .
tear	(tore)	. . . .
whirr	. . . .	. . . .
acquit	acquitted	acquitting
admit	. . . .	. . . .
await	. . . . . .	. . . .
benefit	. . . .	. . . .
budget	. . . .	. . . .
chat	. . . .	. . . .
cheat	. . . .	. . . .

commit	. . . .	. . . .
defeat	. . . .	. . . .
fidget	. . . .	. . . .
fit	. . . . .	. . . . . .
fillet	. . . .	. . . .
float	. . . . . .	. . . .
greet	. . . . . .	. . . .
jut	. . . . .	. . . . . .
knit	. . . . . .	. . . .
meet	(met)	. . . . . .
net	. . . . .	. . . . . .
omit	. . . . . .	. . . .
outwit	. . . .	. . . .
permit	. . . .	. . . .
pilot	. . . . . .	. . . .
pivot	. . . . . .	. . . .
profit	. . . .	. . . .
quit	. . . . . .	. . . .
recruit	. . . .	. . . .
regret	. . . .	. . . .
repeat	. . . .	. . . .
rivet	. . . . . .	. . . .
strut	. . . .	. . . .
submit	. . . .	. . . .
suit	. . . . .	. . . . . .
transmit	. . . .	. . . .
trumpet	. . . .	. . . .
visit	. . . . . .	. . . .
wait	. . . . .	. . . . . .

(see also 4.4.6)

5.1.6   *Complete the spelling of the verbs in the following sentences:*
We have pleasure in a . . . pt . . . your kind invitation.

The employer al . . w . . his employees an extra day's leave at Christmas.

My favourite singer is ap . . . r . . . at the Palladium.

At . . . . . d is a copy of the previous letter, as prom . . . d.

He was unfortunately af . li . t . . with a fit of hi . . . p . . . when tel . . . on . . . his employer who found this rather an . . y . . . , thin . . . . him to have been drin . . . . .

They have manufa . . . r . . a new spar . . . . . drink r . s . mb . . . . champagne.

The bride's father as . . nt . . to his s . . g . st . . . the postp . . . . .
of the wedding until he could be r . l . . s . . from pla . . . . for
Coketown Un . t . . .

While emb . . . d . . . . . the dress she was ma . . . . from a
pattern, the needle p . . r . . . her finger when she was chat . . . . to
her friend without not . . . . . what was hap . . n . . . .

5.2.1   **-age/-ice/-ism/-hood/-ment/-ness/-ship/-ty**
Form nouns ending with one of these suffixes from the following words.
(Note that words ending in **-y** may have to be altered—*see
5.2.2*—and some words will need an **e** or an **i** before the suffix **-ty**:
e.g. gay—gaiety.)

anxious	equal	keen	owner		weary
dark	shrink	child	casual		lonely
special	bond	patriot	fatal	knight	pure
coward	hero	curious	serve		suitable
sudden	fellow	thin	prosper		drunken
festive	various	novel	stupid	real	loyal
able	clever	merry	happy		joyful
parent	active	ready			

5.2.2   **-y**
If the letter before a **y** is a consonant, change the **y** to an **i** when
adding a suffix—except when the suffix is **-ing**
If the letter before the **y** is a vowel, keep the **y** when adding a
suffix (*see also 4.1.1*).
Complete the spellings of the following words with **y** *or* **i**.

tidy	tidier	tidiest	tidily
happy	. . . .	. . . .	happ . ly
weary	. . . .	wear . est	. . . .
merry	. . . . . .	. . . .	. . . .
steady	stead . er	. . . .	. . . .
cry	cried	crying	
fry	. . . . .	. . . . . .	
try	. . . . .	. . . . . .	
carry	carr . es	carr . ed	carr . ing
worry	. . . .	. . . .	. . . .
hurry	. . . .	. . . .	. . . .
rely	. . . . . .	. . . . . .	. . . .
defy	. . . . . .	. . . . . .	. . . .
deny	. . . . .	. . . . . .	. . . .
study	. . . . .	. . . . . .	. . . .
simplify	. . . .	. . . .	. . . .

play	plays	played	playing
delay	dela . .	dela . . .	dela . . . .
destroy	. . . .	. . . .	. . . .
employ	. . . .	. . . .	. . . .
enjoy	. . . . . .	. . . .	. . . .
annoy	. . . . . .	. . . .	. . . .
survey	. . . .	. . . .	. . . .

5.2.3 -ful/-fully

full (and **till**) added to the end of another word drop an l, e.g. useful, handful, until (*see also 4.4.3*).

Complete the following list:

joy	joyful	joyfully
mercy	merciful	. . . .
beauty	. . . .	. . . .
play	. . . .	. . . .
pain	. . . .	. . . .
hope	. . . .	. . . .
shame	. . . .	. . . .
truth	. . . .	. . . .
scorn	. . . .	. . . .
pity	. . . . . .	. . . .
peace	. . . .	. . . .
faith	. . . .	. . . .
respect	. . . .	. . . .
use	. . . . . .	. . . .

5.2.4 -ly

Add **-ly** *to the following words (N.B. see instructions for 5.2.2):*

annual	busy	crooked	especial	exact	final
forceful	full	funny	general	gradual
greedy	grievous	habitual	mere	mortal
mysterious	natural	original	perilous
quiet	real	safe	sincere	speedy	time

5.2.5 Plurals

Some words derived from Old English have retained their plural forms (e.g. man, men; child, children; foot, feet) and words derived from other languages also need care (e.g. from Greek—crisis, crises; criterion, criteria; and from Latin—species, species). Normally, however, the spelling patterns follow these examples:

1 piece, pieces; animal, animals (add **s** only)
2 glass, glasses (if a word ends in an **s**, usually add **-es**)
  church, churches (if a word ends in **-ch**, add **-es**)
  dish, dishes (if a word ends in **-sh**, add **-es**)
  fox, foxes; waltz, waltzes (words ending in **-x**, and **-z** also add **-es**)
3 city, cities (words ending in **y** change to **-ies**)
4 *but* railway, railways; valley, valleys (words ending in **-ay** or **ey** simply add **s**)
5 dwarf, dwarfs—*but* most words change to **-ves**:
  self, selves; calf, calves; loaf, loaves
  Give the plural forms of the following words:

alley	company	opportunity
apology	difficulty	patch
article	dress	pedal
badge	factory	performance
balcony	ferry	piece
berry	genius	potato
bicycle	grocery	quantity
box	guarantee	query
branch	half	radio
bridge	handkerchief	shelf
brush	housewife	storey
bus	inquiry	story
butterfly	knife	thief
ceremony	lady	tomato
chimney	leaf	turkey
cigarette	licence	valley
cliff	lorry	wife
colliery	notice	wish

5.3.1   **-able or ible?**

These endings are often confused. The main patterns are:

use **-able** —after root words, e.g. avail-able, depend-able
      —after root words ending in **e** (drop the **e** as when adding
       a suffix to a verb), e.g. desire—desirable,
       believe—believable, use—usable
      —after **-i**, e.g. reliable, sociable
      —when other forms of the root word have a dominant **a**
       vowel, e.g. irritate—irritable, duration—durable,
       abominate, abomination—abominable
      —after a hard **c** or **g**, e.g. educable, practicable,
       navigable.

Learn these exceptions:

formidable	indomitable	inevitable	memorable
portable	probable		

111

Use **-ible** —after non-word roots, e.g. aud-ible, horr-ible, poss-ible

—when the root has a noun form made by adding the suffix -ion, e.g. suggest, suggestion, suggestible; digest, digestion, digestible; convert, conversion, convertible

—after a root ending in -ns or -miss, e.g. responsible, comprehensible, permissible

—after a soft c or g, e.g. legible, negligible, forcible, invincible.

Learn these exceptions:

contemptible   resistible   collapsible   flexible

Complete the following words with the letter a *or* i *as appropriate:*

admir . ble	plaus . ble
cur . ble	practic . ble
elig . ble	regrett . ble
flex . ble	respect . ble
imagin . ble	respons . ble
imposs . ble	service . ble
indel . ble	tang . ble
indispens . ble	vis . ble
irrit . ble	

Complete the following sentences with words ending -able *or* -ible:

The hovercraft makes it po . . . ble for the modern explorer to approach many previously . . ac . . s . . ble (unable to be reached) areas of the world.

This food's ter . . ble: it's not even e . . ble (fit to be eaten), let alone d . . . . . ble (able to be digested).

Before going to the cinema, the most sen . . ble plan would be to find out if entrance for under-14s is perm . . . . ble (allowable), as it is highly pro . . ble (likely) that the monster effects will be made to appear so b . l . . . . ble (may be believed) that they will be too hor . . ble for our children.

It's . . cr . . . ble (astonishing) how . . . . t . ble (easily excited) football crowds are. We live a mile from the stadium, and every Saturday their roars are clearly . . d . ble (able to be heard), the scoring or failure to score a goal being re . . . n . . . ble (identifiable) by a distinctly not . . . . ble change in pitch and volume. Although the match is . . v . . . ble (incapable of being seen) we can almost follow what is happening without being there.

-er/-or/-ar/-re/-ure

Change the following verbs into nouns by adding the appropriate suffix (check with your dictionary if in doubt):
Example arbitrate—arbitrator

act	collect	commute	conduct	desert
design	inspect	invade	invent	negotiate
operate	organize	prospect		produce
supervise	translate			

Check your answer with the Checklist on pp. 137–70.
Fill the gaps in the following words, which end in -ar or er:

burgl . r	calend . r	. . rcul . r	d . . . ht . r
d . . m . t . r	e . th . r	f . mil . . r	flat . . r
f . rth . r	p . rti . . l . r	p . cu . . . r	pil . . r
pop . . . r	re . ist . r	reg . l . r	rem . . b . r
sla . . ht . r	sp . . dom . t . r		spe . ta . . l . r
transmit . . r	trump . t . r	vin . g . r	vis . t . r
v . lg . r			

Have you noticed the pattern in the spelling of this suffix with most of the adjectives in this list? Check your answers with the Checklist on pp. 137–70, and do likewise after attempting the assignments that follow:
Fill the gaps in these sentences with words ending -ure:

On arriving home from the College of Agr . . . . t . . . , he had to end . . . a l . . t . . . by his father for his f . . l . . . to s . c . . . the front door on his dep . . t . . . that morning. They were lucky not to have had some f . . n . t . . . stolen by a burglar.

The girl was busy attending to her man . c . . . , while her boyfriend waited for her, wondering if they would miss the beginning of the main f . . t . . . film, which opened with a horrific t . . t . . . scene that he was particularly looking forward to.

His firm is going to man . f . . t . . . a new type of pre . s . . . gauge for detecting changes in m . . st . . . content.

Complete the spelling of the following words:
a . q . i . . —to gain
b . w . . . —be on one's guard against
. . nt . . —the middle point of anything
. omp . . . —to set (things) together to ascertain how far they agree or disagree

113

d . . l . . .   —to make known: to assert
e . pl . . .   —to search or travel through for the purpose of discovery
re . . i . .   —to demand: to need
s . v . . .   —rigorous, very strict: unsparing: hard to endure
th . . t . .   —a play-house
th . . . f . . .—for that or this reason
ump . . .   —an impartial person chosen to enforce the rules and decide disputes
in . . . . .   —to seek information

5.3.3   **-ary/-ery/-ory**
Write one word for each of the following definitions:

dis . ipl . n . ry—concerning order maintained by control
disp . n . . ry   —a place where medicines are dealt out in portions
dru . . . ry   —hard or humble labour
. mbr . . d . ry —the art of producing ornamental designs in needlework on textile fabrics, etc.
f . . t . ry   —a place where goods are manufactured
gal . . ry   —a long balcony: an upper floor of seats (esp. in theatre): a room or building for the exhibition of works of art
ima . . n . ry   —not real, non-existent
inv . nt . ry   —a catalogue (listed) stock of goods
lab . r . t . ry   —a place where scientific experiments are systematically carried on
le . . nd . ry   —concerning the activities of a traditional hero, etc.
mig . . t . ry   —wandering: passing from one place to another (e.g. species of birds)
mil . t . ry   —pertaining to soldiers or warfare
mon . st . ry   —a house for monks

Again, make sure you check your answers with the Checklist on pp. 137–70. Words ending in -ery are often obvious (e.g. very, brewery, flattery, bakery, nursery) when spoken, so if in doubt use -ary, when choosing between these two endings, though the following -ery words need noting:

cemetery   confectionery   distillery   dysentery
millinery   monastery   stationery   (paper—note the common e in these two words to distinguish from stationary —still)

Note that each of the words in this assignment has a vowel before -ry: make sure each syllable of the word is included in your spelling of it, thinking first of the pronunciation of the word (e.g. fac-tor-y, gal-ler-y, lab-o-ra-tor-y) before deciding which suffix to use. *Complete the following words (remembering to check your answer carefully and adding any words that cause difficulty to your list of words needing special care):*

an . . v . rs . ry —returning, happening, or commemo-rated, about the same time every year

compul . . ry —obligatory, enforced

confe . . . . n . ry—sweetmeats

e . pl . n . t . ry —serving to explain or clear up

n . . s . ry —an apartment for children: a place where the growth of anything (e.g. plants) is promoted: a school for children aged 2–5

p . . t . ry —earthenware vessels: a place where such goods are manufactured

pr . p . r . t . ry —introductory

pr . . . ry —first: fundamental

satisf . . t . ry —giving contentment

se . . nd . ry —next after the first in time, place, power, quality, etc.

s . . r . t . ry —one employed to conduct corre-spondence and transact business for an individual, society, etc.

sta . . . n . ry —standing: not moving: fixed: perma-nently located

sta . . . n . ry —goods sold by one who sells paper and other goods used in writing

sub . . d . . ry —subordinate

s . r . . ry —consulting room of medical practitioner, dentist, etc.

vet . . . n . ry —pertaining to the art of treating the diseases of domestic animals

5·3·4   -ant/-ent/-ance/-ence
Change the following verbs into nouns by adding the suffix -ance or -ence as appropriate (check with your dictionary if you are not sure), altering the spelling of the stem if necessary:

Example: abstain—abstinence

appear	assure	condole	convey	disturb
endure	enter	exist	insure	offend
precede	pretend	reside	revere	

Change the following verbs into adjectives by adding the suffix -ant *or*
-ent *again altering the spelling of the stem if necessary:*
  Example: abound—abundant
    confide   differ   ignore   obey   suffice

*Add the missing letter to each of these adjectives, then change each word
into a noun by adding the appropriate suffix. Write the pair of adjectives
and nouns in two separate lists, one of words ending* -ant, -ance *the other of
words ending* -ent, -ence:
                              adjective   noun
  Example: abund . nt = abundant, abundance
             ignor . nt = ignorant,   ignorance
             rever . nt = reverent,   reverence
             differ . nt = different, difference
    consequ . nt   conveni . nt   dist . nt   eleg . nt
    emin . nt   fluoresc . nt   fragr . nt   import . nt
    independ . nt   innoc . nt   intellig . nt
    intoler . nt   irrelev . nt   luxuri . nt   magnific . nt
    obedi . nt   observ . nt   obsolesc . nt pati . nt
    penit . nt   perman . nt   pres . nt   promin . nt
    repent . nt   resist . nt   vigil . nt   viol . nt

  The suffix **-ant/-ent** is sometimes also used as the ending of a
noun.
  Example: A depend**ant** (noun) is one who depends on, or is
sustained by, another. A person fillling in an income tax form has to
state if he or she has any depend**ants**—children, invalids or elderly
relations, for instance—who are depend**ent** (adjective) on his or her
income for their food, shelter and clothing, etc.
  Complete the spelling of the following nouns:
    a . . . . nt . nt   —one who keeps, or is skilled in, accounts
    a . . . st . nt   —a helper
    a . . . nd . nt   —one who accompanies, esp. in order to
                          render service
    cl . . m . nt   —one who makes a demand for some-
                          thing supposed due
    co . . . sp . . d . nt —one who keeps in touch with another
                          by writing letters
    cur . . nt   —a small kind of black raisin or dried
                          seedless grape
    cur . . nt   —a flow of air, water or electricity
    inc . d . nt   —an episode
    inf . . m . nt   —one who gives information
    ten . nt   —one who holds or possesses land or
                          property under another: an occupant
    tor . . nt   —a rushing stream (of water, lava, etc.)

Fill the gaps in the following sentences:

Police were called to deal with a dist . . b . n . . in the town centre last night, a v . . l . nt in . . d . nt involving two gangs, the cons . . . . n . . s of which were several arrests for various of . . n . . s and heavy claims for in . . r . n . . by shop-keepers.

It is not s . . fi . . . nt to attend only to the ap . . . r . n . . of your horse: you must also train it to be ob . d . . nt. A horse that is ign . r . nt of how to behave in heavy traffic and has not benefited from the e . p . r . . n . . of p . . . . nt but vi . . l . nt training may be magn . . . . . nt to look at but will be so ind . p . nd . nt of its rider that it will be res . . t . nt to any attempts to restrain it, and thus become a hazard to other road users and lead to dangerous and embarrassing . . r . . mstan . . s for the rider as well.

(*Check your answers with the Checklist, as before.*)

Revision Exercises

Fill the gaps in the words listed below:

abil . ty	thre . t . n . d	c . . mut . r
anx . . ty	tot . l . ed	d . si . ner
fact . ry	cel . bra . . . n	man . ger
inq . . ry	exa . . . ra . . . n	nego . . . tor
secr . t . ry	exam . na . . . n	op . r . t . r
var . . ty	s . . . est . . n	conven . . nt
hap . . ness	c . ura . . . us	ign . r . nt
re . d . ness	spa . . . us	import . nt
sud . e . ness	obv . . us	in . . d . nt
we . r . ness	a . . oying	magnif . . . nt
a . . . mpan . ed	a . . e . ling	obed . . nt
a . . no . l . . ged	compl . ting	pa . . . nt
admit . ed	. njoying	v . . l . nt
beg . ed	ex . it . . g	grocery, grocer . . s
car . . ed	expres . . . g	lorry, lorr . . s
compe . . ed	fas . inat . . g	notice, notic . s
con . . ered	fit . . ng	valley, vall . . s
d . stro . . d	hur . . ing	b . l . . v . ble
dis . . p . . nted	not . . ing	man . g . . ble
ent . r . d	pers . . ding	pos . . ble
patrol . . d	prep . . ing	r . spons . ble
pr . fer . . d	q . ar . . . ling	
r . gret . . d	re . . . nising	
re . . ired	suf . . ring	
sat . sf . ed	vis . ting	
strug . . . d		

appe . r . n . e   cons . q . . ntly   saf . ly
co . . . spond . n . e fa . thfu . . y   sin . . r . ly
di f . . r . n . e   fin . . . y   tr . . y
ins . r . n .e   grad . . . ly
serv . . e   gr . . v . usly
be . ut . fu . ly   myster . . usly

6   Spelling—roots and prefixes

"When Francis Bacon (1561–1626) referred to various people in the course of his *Essays* as 'indifferent', 'obnoxious', and 'officious', he was describing them as 'impartial', 'submissive', and 'Ready to serve'. When King James II observed that the new St Paul's Cathedral was 'amusing' 'awful', and 'artificial', he implied that Sir Christopher Wren's recent creation was 'pleasing, awe-inspiring, and skilfully achieved.' When Dr Johnson (1709–84) averred that Milton's poem *Lycidas* was 'easy, vulgar, and therefore disgusting' he intended to say that it was 'effortless, popular, and therefore not in good taste.'"

(Simeon Potter, *Our Language*)

6.1   Modern English has evolved over a thousand years of constant use, and our present spelling reflects the changes that have occurred in our language. Just as the appearance of the town or village in which you live has been changed over the centuries by the different demands people have made of it (and are still making), so the words we speak and write have been modified too. For instance, think about the invasions of the British Isles by Romans, Vikings, and Normans, or of the expansion of Britain's Empire in the sixteenth to nineteenth centuries, and you will soon find reasons for these changes. Remember also that 'English' is used by millions of people all over the world as a first or second language (as you read this perhaps the navigating crew of a jet airliner arriving at Cairo from Moscow will be calling up the control tower in English, English may be being spoken at the United Nations Assembly by an African politician, by scientists at an international conference, by businessmen and technicians . . .). English, its pronunciation and spelling will continue to adapt to these circumstances too. A good dictionary will help you to see the history of some of these changes, helping you to understand why some apparently contradictory spellings have come about (for instance, why we spell 'fitted' with two ts and 'benefited' with one).

6.1.1   Look up the meaning of *etymology*. Find an etymological dictionary in your library. Why is it etymologically inaccurate to refer to a wooden shed as being 'dilapidated' or a battalion as being 'well equipped'? How have the meanings of 'governor', 'marshal', 'constable', 'companion', 'fellow', 'comrade', and 'friend' been altered from their original definitions?

What is common about the changes in meanings that have occurred in these words:

crafty	meat	deer	fowl	hound	disease
starve	wed	affection	lessons		science
undertaker	doctor	silly	nice?		

6.1.2   *Give as many examples as you can to show how these words can have several meanings:*

cataract	head	line	paper	pipe	place
power					

6.1.3   *Many of our words are derived from Latin and Greek. Which languages do these words come from?*

bazaar	bandit	bungalow	cigar	caravan
balcony	garage	sofa	tea	yacht	trek
loot	jungle			

6.1.4   *Use an etymological dictonary to find out the answers to these questions:*

What is the connection between *cereal* and a goddess? (What is the difference between this word and its homonym *serial*?)

Why is the fruit, etc., served after a meal referred to as *dessert*?

What is *foolscap*, and how did it get its name?

Which words have been combined to give the word *fortnight*?

Why are *italics* so called?

What was the original meaning of *neighbour*?

What does the prefix *step-* mean in the words stepson, stepdaughter, etc.?

What, strictly speaking, is the purpose of an *umbrella*?

6.1.5   *Here are dictionary definitions of modern words whose roots are in Old English (O.E.). By referring to the list of O.E. words can you work out which words are being defined?*

Not often

Sour, sharp or painful

A man to whom a woman is married
A passage between rows of seats
A container for carrying water, etc.
Firm, constant, and unchanging

Bitan (to bite)   gangan (to go)   fretan (to eat)   hus
(house)   seld (rare)   stede (place)

6.1.6   *Here are some French words. Do they remind you of English words with a
similar (not necessarily exactly the same) meaning and spelling?*

ami (friend)   mur (wall)
année (year)   nom (name)
blanc (white)   orner (decorate)
comprendre (understand)   pensée (thought)
donner (give)   petit (small)
digne (worthy)   pendre (hang)
dormir (sleep)   terminer (finish)
escalier (staircase)   utile (useful)
femme (woman)   temps (time)
fil (thread)   terre (earth)
lumière (light)

You may be able to think of several English words related to each of
the words in this list: check with your dictionary to see if there are
any you have overlooked.

6.1.7   *Here are some Latin words. Can you think of English words derived from
them?*

alter (the other of two)   gradus (a step or degree)
erro (wander, stray)   gratus (pleasing, thankful)
fames (hunger)   rota (a wheel)
locus (a place)   tremo (shake, quiver)
                                vagor (wander)

*Look up the first three letters of each of these words in your dictionary. Can
you find further words derived from the same root? Which English words are
derived from these roots?*

credo (believe)   frigus (cold)   migro (remove, depart to
another place)   numerus (number)   operis (work)
porto (carry)   ruptum (break)   tribuo (give)

6.1.8 *Add one or more of the following prefixes (see 6.2) to the roots in 6.1.7 to make up further words:*

in-   co-   trans-   im-   re-   e-   dis-   con-
inter-

6.1.9 *Look up words beginning with the following groups of letters:*

ambul	geo (and terra)	quad
ante		
anti	junct	scri
aqua		spec
audi	magn (and mega)	
	manu	tele
auto	mon(o) (and sol)	temp
bio		ten
	paci	tract
chron	ped	tri
circum	peri	
corp	phil	voca
cruc	phos (and phot)	vis
	prim	
fin	punct	
flu		

Can you work out what these roots mean?

Which words are referred to in the following definitions? (The root will not necessarily appear at the beginning of a word):

A lever moved by the *foot*
To make *peace*ful and quiet; to soothe
The science of plant and animal *life*
Great in deeds or show: grand: noble
Uttered in *one*, unvaried tone
Alone, without company
Cannot be *seen*
To *draw* (to), cause to approach
Able to be *heard*
A *cycle with three* wheels
A *foot*-passenger
A vehicle used for haulage, or for *draw*ing ploughs, etc.
To cause to appear *greater*
A hole made by a sharp *point*
An assembly of *hearer*s
A space enclosed by *three* straight lines
Exact in keeping time or appointments (arriving 'on the *dot*')
To *draw* out by force, to take
That can be *seen*; clear to the mind; obvious
Lasting, used, for a *time* only

To go at a slow *walking*-pace
A *written* direction for the preparation of medicine
Care of the *hands* and finger-nails
To over*see*, to superintend
An account of anything in words
One who lives at the same *time*: present day (an inaccurate use), esp. up to date, fashionable
To *look* into, to examine
To make, originally by *hand*, now usually by machinery
Belonging to the beginning, or to the *first* times: original: ancient
An instrument for reproducing sound, esp. speech, *at a distance*
*Join*ing, union, or combination: place or point of union
The science that describes the surface of the *earth* and its inhabitants
One who *holds* or possesses land or property under another: an occupant

6.2   *Prefix*—a particle or word put before a word to affect its meaning.
   Example: pre—before, previous to
      Precaution —caution or care beforehand
      Prearrange —to arrange beforehand
      Precede   —to go before in time, rank, or importance
      Predict   —to foretell

A prefix differs from a suffix in its effect on the spelling of a root word or stem. As has been shown earlier in this book, a suffix may alter the spelling of the root word:
      appear, appeared, appearing, appearance—no change;
      satisfy, satisfying (no change), satisfied—y change to i before suffix beginning with a vowel (two is are rare in English);
      approve, approved approving—the silent e is dropped.

The meaning of each of these words could be changed by adding the prefix **dis-** but adding a prefix to a word does not affect its spelling:
      dis + appear = disappear;   dis + approve = disapprove;
      dis + satisfy = dissatisfy.

Therefore think of the spelling of the prefix, and simply add it to the word.

6.2.1   The word 'impatient' means *not* patient. Other prefixes that mean *not* are **il-, in-, ir-,** and **un-.**

Complete the following sentences with the correct prefix:

These tools are cheaper than those: they are really quite . . expensive.

I don't believe that: it sounds . . probable to me.

He was prosecuted for having an . . accurate speedometer.

Her . . regular attendance at the clinic worried the doctor.

I hope it isn't . . convenient for you.

They were generous, kind, and . . selfish in their attitude.

A stain made the specimen . . perfect.

He doesn't know what to do: he's completely . . decided.

I'm . . certain about the correct answer.

Parking a car at a road-junction is . . legal.

The roots were wedged under the wall: the tree was . . movable.

The old man was . . firm and too weak to leave his bed.

It is . . possible for me to come.

His . . polite behaviour was completely . . tolerable.

The vicar thought the joke was . . reverent.

6.2.2   *Complete the spelling of the following words, which all end in* -al *and begin with a prefix meaning* not:

il . . gal	—not lawful
il . . . . . al	—contrary to the rules of logic
im . . t . . . al	—unimportant
im . . . al	—inconsistent with what is right: wicked
im . . . . al	—exempt from death: imperishable: never to be forgotten
imp . . . . al	—not favouring one more than another: just
in . . v . . . al	—opposite to general: special, particular
in . . s . . . . al	—not necessary

(After completing each assignment in this chapter, make sure you check your answers with the complete spellings in the Checklist on pp. 137–70.)

6.2.3   *The following words end in -nt. Complete their spellings (as in 6.2.2):*

incon . . s . . nt	—changeable, fickle: not suitable or agreeing (with)
incon . . n . . nt	—causing trouble or difficulty
inco . . r . nt	—loose, rambling
ind . . . nt	—offensive to common modesty or propriety
ind . . . nt	—lazy
ind . p . nd . nt	—not relying on others: thinking or acting for oneself
ins . l . nt	—insulting: rude
ins . . f . . . . nt	—not enough
infr . . . . nt	—seldom occurring
in . o . . nt	—not hurtful: harmless: blameless: ignorant of evil
imp . . . . nt	—lacking patience
imp . . . nt	—wanting shame or modesty

(See also 5.3.4)

6.2.4   *The following words end in -te. Complete their spellings (as in 6.2.2–3):*

im . . c . l . te	—spotless: pure: unstained
im . . d . . te	—with nothing between: without delay
im . . l . te	—uncivil
inc . mp . . te	—insufficient
inc . ns . d . . . te	—not mindful of the claims of others: rash: thoughtless
ind . sc . . m . . . te	—not distinguishing relative merits (e.g. praise or blame)
inf . n . te	—without end or limit

6.2.5   *In each of the following sentences the words to be completed begin with a prefix meaning* not *and have the same final two letters:*

The team of doctors and nurses have an . . m . n . . (that cannot be measured: vast in extent) task trying to . . m . n . . . (to render free from danger of infection) thousands of nomads, many of whom may have moved to other parts of the country already.

She had been given a length of material that was . . p . r . . . . (falling short of perfection), and was angry when the manager of the shop tried to tell her that she was . . . . r . . . . (not accurate, wrong), saying that the . . d . st . . . . (not plainly marked) pattern at the end of the roll was deliberate.

Her uncle tried to explain to her cousin that she was not an

. . s . n . . . . (deceitful) person, merely . . m . t . . . . (showing marks of incomplete development) and also rather . . s . c . . . (unsure of herself) after the death of her parents.

At the sales there were many women behaving in a very . . d . . is . . . manner, finding it impossible to choose between so many tempting and . . e . pen . . . . goods.

6.2.6   *Complete the gaps in the following adjectives (see 3.3.6) that begin with the prefix* im- *or* in- *and have a common suffix (see 4.1) also. The root words from which the adjectives are formed are given in brackets.*
Example: in . . . . able (operate) = in*o*p*e*rable
　　　　im . . . able (move)
　　　　im . . . . able (Latin verb peccare—to sin)
　　　　im . . . . able (practise)
　　　　in . . . . . . able (compare)
　　　　in . . . able (cure)
　　　　in . . . . . able (define)
　　　　in . . . . . . able (dispute)
　　　　in . . . . able (Latin verb, vitare—to avoid)
　　　　in . . . . . able (excuse)
　　　　in . . . . . . able (Latin ex—out + verb plicare—to fold)
　　　　in . . . . . able (Latin adjective numerabilis—that can be counted)
　　　　il . . . ible (Latin verb legere—to read)
　　　　im . . . . ible (perceive)
　　　　in . . . . ible (Latin verb credere—to believe)
　　　　in . . . . ible (destroy)
　　　　in . . ible (Latin verb edere—to eat)
　　　　in . . . . ible (Latin verb elegere—to choose from)
　　　　in . . . . ible (Latin verb fallere—to deceive)
　　　　in . . . . ible (Latin verb flectere—to bend)
　　　　in . . . ible (Latin verb videre—to see)

6.2.7   *Fill the gaps in the following sentences with words beginning with the prefix* im- *or* in-. *(The meaning of the prefixes is different from that in 6.2.1–6):*
Her teacher told her parents that he was very impr . . . . d by their daughter's progress: she had done well this term, and her work showed signs of a marked impro . . . . nt.

The surgeon picked up a shining impl . . . nt to make a neat in . . s . . n in the patient's chest, ind . . . ting to the students the intri . . t . structure of the int . r . . r of the human body as he did so. He inv . . . d them to make a thorough insp . . . . . n of the diseased area, showing them how it had in . re . . . d since the last operation, and giving instr . . . . . ns on the correct procedure for removing the damaged tissue.

The firm's int . n . . . n is to int . . d . . . a new model in the Spring—when, in . . d . nt . . . y, their main rival hopes to make a big imp . . t on the market too. The continual intr . g . . s of car manufacturers can be most in . en . . . s, their advertising campaigns using the im . . . n . t . v . talents of the designers to the full, hoping to impr . . . us with the speed and power of their product.

"The trouble with you is that you are far too imp . t . . . s, ind . . d you always seem to be rushing into things without thinking, always acting on some crazy imp . l . ., inst . . d of stopping to think about what might happen afterwards. No wonder the police think you were impl . . . . . d in that robbery: you've been invo . . . d in in . . d . n . . like that before. If you were more inte . l . . . nt, you'd keep yourself out of trouble." It was obvious that his mother was inf . r . . t . d with his behaviour. She was in . . n . . d with rage, fearing that his arrest by the police was im . . n . nt.

The fire officer hoped they were thoroughly ins . . . d against danger to their stock, which contained many highly infl . . . . . . materials.

6.2.8   'Confuse' is made up of the prefix **con-**, which, like **co-** and **com-**, means 'with' or 'together', and the root word 'fuse' (meaning to melt one thing with another by heat—hence, to blend, merge)
Find words beginning with these prefixes to fit the following definitions:

co-op . . . . . —to work together (towards some end)
conv . . . . n —talk, familiar discourse with another person or persons
con . r . . . —formed into one mass: a mixture of lime, sand, pebbles, etc.
cont . . . t —scorn, disgrace
cont . n . . . . —joined together without interruption
cont . n . . . —unceasing: very frequent
con . e s . . . n —an accumulation causing obstruction
com . . n . . . . . —to make known: to exchange information by letter, etc.: to succeed in conveying one's meaning to others
col . . . t —to assemble or bring together: to gather
co-in . . . . —to occupy the same space or time: to be identical: to agree (with)

coal	—to grow together or to unite into one body
comp . . .	—any assembly of persons: a number of persons associated together for trade, etc.
comp . . ment	—an expression of praise, or of respect
comp . . .	—to write or compose by collecting the materials from other books: to draw up or collect
conc . . .	—to make up (as a dish in cookery); to fabricate (e.g. a story)
con . . . t	—to tie or fasten together
conde . .	—to pronounce guilty: to censure or blame

Complete the gaps in the following sentences with words beginning with these prefixes:

The engineer went to the hospital to visit his col . . . g . . (one associated with another in a profession or occupation) who had only just regained con . . . . . . n . . . (the state of having awareness or knowledge) after an accident three days before caused by the col . . p . . (falling or breaking down) of a wall after a crane had col . . d . . with a lorry passing the con . . . led (hidden) entrance to the site. As he walked along the cor . . d . . (a passage-way or gallery communicating with separate rooms, etc.) leading to the ward, he thought about the strange co-in . . d . . . . (the occurrence of one event at the same time as, or following another, without any causal connection) that a year ago on the same day he had been taken to hospital suffering from con . . s . . . . (a condition produced by a heavy blow, esp. on the head) after a similar accident. Surely their firm would comp . . (force) all employees to observe the safety regulations in future? There had been many compl . . . ts (expressions of dissatisfaction) recently.

After a long discussion, during which many useful com . . n . . (remarks, observations, criticisms) had been conv . . . d (imparted, communicated) from both sides, the joint com . . . t . . (a number of persons, selected from a more numerous body, to whom some special business is committed) decided as a comp . . m . . . (a settlement of differences by mutual concession) to comb . . . (to join together in one whole: to unite closely) the fund-raising activities of the various societies, hoping that by col . . b . r . . . .g (working in association) their efforts towards a com . . n (belonging equally to more than one:

general) purpose they would be able to col . . . t (gather) enough money to build a new com . . n . . . (the public in general) centre near the F.E. Col . . . . . Everyone present at the meeting cons . . t . . (agreed to give assent to) to this proposal, and it was decided to com . . n . . (begin: originate) the campaign immediately, con . . . t . . . ing (directing with a single purpose or intention: focus) on raising enough money initially to lay the con . r . . . foundations. The con . l . . . . n (end, last part) of the meeting was a brief speech by the Mayor, who said that the new building was the con . . . n (that which affects or interests) of everybody and that he was pleased that all parties had agreed to co- . p . r . . . (work together).

After cong . . t . . . . ing (expressing joyful sympathy) the group on the success of their con . . . t (a musical entertainment), their manager announced that after a long cor . . . p . . d . . . . (communicating, esp. by letter) with the record comp . . . (a number of persons associated together for trade) he had negotiated a new cont . . . t (an agreement on fixed terms: a bond) which would com . . . (force) any record producer to pay them an additional fee for their own comp . . . . . . ns (creations, esp. in music), as well as performance fees.

6.2.9   The prefix **dis-** has a similar effect on words as that shown by the prefixes in 6.2.1.

Example: honour = high estimation: any mark of respect or esteem;
dishonour = shame: disgrace (note the prefix having the same effect in this word)
As with other prefixes, **dis-** does not affect the spelling of the word to which it is fixed: so just as the opposite of 'logical' is formed by adding the prefix il- (illogical), or of 'moral' by adding im- (immoral), so **dis** + appear = disappear and **dis** + satisfy = dissatisfy.
Complete the spellings of the following words that begin with this prefix:

dis . . . . d	—crippled
disg	—a false appearance
dis . . . . . t	—to cleanse from infection
disint	—to separate into parts; to crumble
dis . . . t	—to cut into parts for minute examination
dis . . m . . . r	—unlike
dis . . l . .	—to melt
dis . . . d .	—to prevent or deter by advice or persuasion

disp . . . .   —to deal out in portions (e.g. a chemist preparing medicines from a doctor's prescription)

Fill the gaps in the following passage with words beginning with this prefix:
The Headteacher met several teachers to . . . c . . s (debate) a pupil. Most of them showed their obvious . . . l . . . (aversion, disapproval) of the boy, calling him . . . . b . . . . nt (neglecting, or refusing to obey), ... n . st (disposed to cheat) and . . . r . p . . v . (causing a breach of discipline). His behaviour was . . . gr . . . f . . (causing shame) and often . . . g . . . ing (loathsome, nauseating), and he should be . . . m . . . . d (expelled) from school for causing such widespread . . . t . . b . . . . (tumult, disorder). A few teachers . . . . g . . . d (differed, dissented), saying that this view was exaggerated, a . . . t . r . . . n (misrepresentation) of the truth: one should . . . . rim . n . . . (make a difference or distinction) between deliberate misbehaviour and the signs of a toubled home life—for instance, the boy was very . . . h . . . t . . . d (discouraged, depressed) by the sudden . . . . p . . . r . . . . (removal from sight, secret withdrawal) of his father. The Headmaster stressed the need for the utmost . . . cr . . . . n (need to be prudent, tactful), and added that he would . . . . p . . . v . (have an unfavourable opinion) of any member of Staff who attempted to . . . o . . (refuse to acknowledge as belonging to oneself, cast off, disclaim) the boy: such an attitude would be a far greater . . . . st . . (calamity) for the school than any damage the boy might cause. The pupil ‗ had a record . . . t . . g . . . . . d (characterized, set apart from others) by repeated . . . pl . . s (exhibitions) of bad behaviour, but compassion might be more effective than punishment. After the meeting had . . . p . . s . d (separated), some of the teachers expressed their . . . . . tisf . . . . . n (state of being discontented), saying they were . . . . p . . . n . . d (their hopes were not fulfilled) by the Headteacher, and would certainly refuse to teach the boy in future. This is how a . . . p . . . (quarrel) began that led to a thousand pupils being sent home from school and a threat of a national strike.

7   Spelling—double check

7.1   *Complete the missing letters in the following words, which are listed alphabetically, then check your answers against the Checklist:*

7.1.1

ac . ur . t .	be . . t . ful	cel . br . ty
a . ros .	ben . . th	cem . t . ry
a . ja . . nt	b . c . cle	cent . ry
an . . ent	b . rthday	cert . . n
ans . . r	Brit . . n	certif . c . t .
apol . . ise	b . s . ness	c . ar . . ter
ap . . opr . . te	campa . . n	choc . l . te
artic . .	can . e . lation	cig . ret . .
attem . t	car . . . ge	c . rcul . r
attend . nt	cas . . l	c . rc . mstan . .
ava . l . ble	cat . log . .	coin . . d . nce
a . k . ard	cat . stro . . ic	col . . ps .ble
basic . . ly		

7.1.2

col . is . . n	cons . . . n . e	cur . . . sly
comf . rt . ble	cons . q . ently	dam . . e
com . un . c . te	consid . r . te	de . lt
c . mp . ny	conta . n . r	d . fe . t
compar . s . n	conv . . sation	def . n . t . ly
compuls . ry	convin . ing	delib . r . te
compl . ment . ry	cor . . spond . n . e	d . si . n . r
compr . mise	cor . . d . r	d . str . ying
con . entrate	c . . rag . . us	d . t . rmin . d
con . lus . . n	c . urt .sy	devel . p . . nt
con . ret .	crit . . . sm	dif . . r . nt
conduct . r	cu . b . . rd	dif . . . ult

disa . t . . . s

dis . . plin .

dis . us . . . n

dise . se

disgra . . ful

disint . . rate

disti . . . ished

e . rl . . r

e . s . ly

ef . i . . . nt

electr . . . ty

empl . y . r

ent . . nce

eq . . pm . nt

espe . . . ly

ev . . yone

ex . . l . . nt

ex . . t . ment

ex . r . ise

expen . iv .

exper . . n . e

extrav . g . nt

f . . thful

fas . . nating

fash . . n . ble

fav . . r . te

fe . t . re

Feb . . . ry

fem . nin .

fic . . on

finan . . al

fl . . res . . nt

for . . gn

fort . n . te

fre . . . ntly

fr . . ndly

fri . . ten . d

fur . . . sly

furn . t . r .

gar . ge

g . . ge

gen . r . . ly

gen . r . . s

g . v . r . ment

gra . . . us

g . . r . ntee

g . . lty

han . . . rch . . f

he . lthy

he . v . ly

hor . . ble

hum . r . . s

h . p . crit . c . l

ident . c . l

ima . . n . ry

im . . d . . t . ly

impa . . . nt

in . . dent . . ly

ind . pend . nt

ind . vid . . l

infe . . . ous

ins . . fi . . . nt

ins . r . nce

intel . . g . nt

int . resting

intr . c . te

intr . du . e

inv . r . . bly

inven . . . n

invis . ble

ir . . l . v . nt

j . . rney

ki . . hen

. no . king

kn . . l . . ge

labor . t . ry

lang . . ge

l . . sure

lib . . ry

lis . . ning

lon . l . n.:ss

lux . ry

ma . . . n . ry

magnif . . . nt

ma . nt .n . nce

man . g . . ble

man . . uvre

man . fa . . . rer

mater . . l

me . s . ring

me . . an . c . l

med . . in .

Med . . . . ran . an

min . . t . re

mis . . . lan . . . s

misch . . . ous

mount . . n

m . ster . . . s

nat . r . . ly

nec . . s . ry

n . . . . bour

not . . ed

num . rous

obed . . nt

obv . . us

ori . . n . . ly

ox . . en

p . rtic . l . rly

pe . . . ful

p . . ul . . r

pe . ple

p . rform . n . e

perm . n . nt

p . rs . ver . n . e

p . rs . . s . . n

po . ket

picni . . ing

p . . s . n . . s

pop . l . r

pos . . bil . ty

pre . . . us

pre . . stor . .

prep . r . tion

prev . . . sly

prin . . p . . ly   p . r p . se   rea . t . . n
priv . l . ge   q . . r . . l   re . d . ly
prob . . ly   qu . . e   re . . ly
pro . e . . re   q . . st . . n refle . . . ion
produ . er   q . . . kly   re . s . n . bly
psy . . ological   radic . . ly

7.1.6

re . . ntly   se . r . t . ry   sur . . ry
re . . . nise   s . c . r . ly   s . . pris . . g
re . . . mend   sep . r . te   s . st . matic
reg . l . rly   sens . b . .   tel . . . one
rej . . . ing   seq . . n . .   temp . . . t . re
rel . t . v . ly   s . ve . . ly   th . r . . . h
reli . . . us   sil . ntly   tra . . dy
relu . t . ntly   sil . o . et . .   tr . . b . .
reme . . . ring   spa . . . us   us . . . ly
rep . t . . . on   spe . ta . . l . r   ve . . t . b . .
r . sist . n . e   ste . d . ly   vet . . . n . ry
r . spe . t . ble   st . m . c .   vil . . ge
r . spon . . b . .   stre . . th   v . . l . nt
r . . thm   strug . . ing   vis . b . .
sat . sfa . t . ry   su . fi . . . nt   vis . t . r
scar . . ly   su . gest   we . r . ly
s . . entifi .   s . rfa . .

7.2   Fill the gaps in the following words with one letter—single or repeated.
Example: a—ey = abbey or alley; mo—ey = money

7.2.1
a—reviation   a—ress   a—oyance
a—eleration   admi—ion   a—ounce
acce—ible   a—ectionate   a—ologizing
a—ident   a—reement   a—ealing
acco—odation   a—owed   a—pointment
acco—paniment   a—oud   a—reciation
a—ountant   a—right   a—roach
accu—ulation   a—ready   a—est
accu—ate   a—ways   a—istant
a—ross   a—iversary   assu—ance

7.2.2
begi—ing   cance—ation   choo—ing
benefi—ing   carefu—   co—aborating
bo—owing   ca—ying   co—iery
bri—iant   ch—rfu—y   co—ing

co—i—ee

concu—ion

confu—ing

co—ect

contro—ing

co-o—erating

co—osion

decli—ing

de—erting

di—e—ent

disa—earance

di—aster

di—mi—ing

di—atisfy

di—olving

emba—a—ment

e—igrate

e—ergency

e—abling

ente—ing

equa—y

7.2.3

exa—erate

explai—ing

fai—ing

fea—ing

fidge—ing

fina—y

fla—ering

fo—owed

forgo—en

fulfi—ment

ga—oping

gree—ing

gue—ing

ha—ening

hei—ess

helpfu—y

hesita—ing

hi—uping

hi—eous

hu—ying

i—egal

i—ustration

imita—ing

i—inent

impo—ible

increa—ing

incu—able

ine—icient

inevit—ble

i—umerable

inte—uption

into—erant

i—egular

irre—istible

l—sing

mee—ing

men—ed

7.2.4

o—a—ionally

o—upation

o—icer

o—ening

o—ortunity

pa—a—el

pa—enger

patro—ing

permi—ion

perso—al

po—e—ion

practi—ing

prefe—ence

pre—ure

progre—

propo—al

prospe—ity

rea—ize

sci—ors

signa—ing

simi—ar

ski—fu—

socia—y

spoi—ing

stea—ing

su—e—fu—y

su—enly

ti—ily

to—ether

transfe—ing

transla—ing

trave—ing

transmi—ing

umbre—a

u—ece—ary

usefu—y

va—ey

w—llen

wri—ling

wri—ing

wri—en

7.3.1 *Complete the following list of verbs, giving the past tense, present participle, and also add a noun formed from the verb by adding a suffix:*

verb	past	present participle (i.e. ending -ing)	noun
Example: annoy=	annoyed	annoying	annoyance
announce	announced	announcing	announcer
			announcement
apologize	apologized	apologizing	apology

achieve	deceive	perceive
apply	declare	permit
appoint	describe	persevere
appreciate	disappoint	please
argue	disapprove	possess
arrive	dissect	practise
assemble	divide	prefer
associate	exceed	produce
behave	frighten	progress
bore	inspect	receive
break	interfere	recognize
bury	interpret	recur
cancel	introduce	refer
coincide	irritate	remember
collect	know	replace
commence	obey	reside
compare	occupy	rob
connect	occur	separate
consider	operate	succeed
		suggest

7.3.2 *Form adjective and adverbs from the following nouns.*
  Example: affection =affectionate, affectionately
      brilliance=brilliant, brilliantly

beauty	care	clumsiness	comfort
completion	consciousness		consequence
co-operation	courage	curiosity	courtesy
definition	disgrace	ease	efficiency	entirety
extent	faith	fortune	fun	gratitude
grace	guilt	hope	inadequacy	inconsideration
mystery	necessity	occasion	origin
prosecution	reluctance	safety	separation
similarity	sincerity	skill	society	success
truth	variety		

7·3·3   *Complete the following words with* ei *or* ie:

aud . . nce   bel . . f   c . . ling   ch . . f   conc . . t
dec . . ve   . . ther   for . . gn   forf . . t   l . . sure
misch . . f   n . . ther   rec . . pt   r . . gn   s . . ze   v . . l
w . . rd

7·3·4   *Add the suffix* -able *or* -ible *to the following verbs, altering their spelling where necessary:*

accept   admire   admit   collapse   conceive
consider   distinguish   divide   eat   elect
enjoy   irritate   perceive   permit   practice
recognize   regret   rely   vary

7·3·5   *Make up sentences that will show you understand the different meanings of the words in the following pairs:*

advice, advise	heal, heel
allowed, aloud	hear, here
angel, angle	hoard, horde
ascent, assent	its, it's
bare, bear	meat, meet
bean, been	mist, missed
berry, bury	of, off
boar, bore	passed, past
board, bored	peace, piece
brake, break	practice, practise
brought, bought	principal, principle
buy, by	quiet, quite
coarse, course	right, write
cloths, clothes	their, there
council, counsel	waist, waste
chord, cord	weather, whether
currant, current	were, where
diner, dinner	your, you're
gorilla, guerilla	
groan, grown	

8 Spelling—checklist

A

abbey: 4.2.3

abbreviate abbreviated abbreviating abbreviation: 3.3.1 7.2.1

able ability: 4.2.3 5.2.1 5.4

abominable: 5.3.1

above: 4.3.9

accelerate accelerated accelerating acceleration: 4.4.1 4.6.4 7.2.1

accept accepted accepting acceptable acceptance: 3.3.2 5.1.1 5.1.6 7.3.4

access accessible: 3.1 7.2.1

accident accidental accidentally: 4.6.1 7.2.1

accommodate accommodated accommodating accommodation: 3.1 4.4.1 4.6.4 7.2.1

accompany accompanied accompanying accompaniment: 3.3.2 3.3.5 5.1.3 5.4 7.2.1

accomplish accomplished accomplishing: 5.1.3

account accounted accounting accountant: 5.3.4 7.2.1

accumulate accumulated accumulating accumulation: 4.4.1 4.6.4 7.2.1

accurate accurately accuracy: 4.6.1 7.1.1 7.2.1

ache ached aching: 3.2.1 4.1.2 4.6.4

achieve achieved achieving achievement: 4.2.1 7.3.1

acknowledge acknowledged acknowledging acknowledg(e)ment: 5.1.3 5.4

across: 3.2.1 4.6.4 7.1.1 7.2.1

acquire acquired acquiring: 5.1.3 5.3.2

acquit acquitted acquitting acquittal: 5.1.5

act acted acting active activity activities action actor: 4.2.3 4.6.1 4.6.2 5.1.2 5.2.1 5.3.2

address addressed addressing: 3.3.2 7.2.1

adjacent: 3.2.2 7.1.1

admire admired admiring admirable admirably admiration: 5.3.1 7.3.4

admit admitted admitting admissible admittedly admission: 3.3.1 4.4.5 4.4.6 5.1.5 5.4 7.2.1 7.3.4

advertise advertised advertising advertisement: 3.3.1
advise advised advising advisable advice (noun): 3.2.4 7.3.5
affect affected affecting affectionate affectionately affection: 3.3.6
  4.6.3 5.1.2 7.2.1
afflict afflicted afflicting affliction: 5.1.6
again: 4.6.2
agree agreed agreeing agreeable agreeably agreement: 3.1 3.3.2
  3.3.7 7.2.1
agriculture: 5.3.2
air aired airing: 5.1.5
ahead: 4.2.4
aisle: 4.1.1
alive: 4.3.9
all: 4.4.3
alley alleys: 4.2.3 5.2.5
allow allowed allowing allowable allowance: 3.2.4 4.6.3 5.1.1 5.1.6
  7.2.1 7.3.5
aloud: 3.2.7 4.6.3 7.2.1 7.3.5
already: 4.4.3 7.2.1
all right: 7.2.1
also: 4.4.3
alter altered altering alteration: 5.1.5
although: 4.4.3
always: 3.3.6 4.6.2 7.2.1
amount: 3.1
ancient: 4.2.1 4.4.1 4.4.5 4.6.4 7.1.1
angel (=divine messenger, pronounced ān'jel): 4.1.1 7.3.5
angle (=the point from which lines/surfaces diverge, pronounced
  ang'gl): 4.1.1 7.3.5
anniversary anniversaries: 5.3.3 7.2.1
announce announced announcing announcer announcement:
  3.3.2 7.2.1
annoy annoyed annoying annoyance: 3.3.4 5.1.6 5.2.2 5.4 7.2.1
annual annually: 5.2.4
answer: 7.1.1
antecedent (=previous, preceding event/circumstance): 4.2.2
anxious anxiety: 5.2.1 5.4
any anything: 4.1.1 4.2.3
apologis(z)e apologis(z)ed apologis(z)ing apology apologies: 3.3.2
  5.2.5 7.1.1 7.2.1
appal appalled appalling: 4.4.6
appeal appealed appealing: 4.4.6 5.1.4 5.4 7.2.1
appear appeared appearing appearance: 4.4.6 4.6.2 5.1.6 5.3.4
  5.4
apply applied applying appliance application: 3.3.4 3.3.5 7.3.1
appoint appointed appointing appointment: 4.4.6 7.2.1 7.3.1

appreciate appreciated appreciating appreciable appreciably
appreciative appreciation: 3.3.2 3.3.7 4.4.6 7.2.1 7.3.1
approach approached approaching: 4.6.1 7.2.1
appropriate: 4.6.1 7.1.1
arbitrate arbitrated arbitrating arbitrator arbitration: 4.6.1 5.3.2
argue argued arguing arguable argument: 3.1 4.1.4 5.1.1 5.1.3
7.3.1
arrest arrested arresting: 4.6.2 7.2.1
arrive arrived arriving arrival: 4.6.2 7.3.1
article articles: 3.3.1 5.2.5 7.1.1
ascent (=climb): 3.2.3 4.6.3 7.3.5
asleep: 4.4.2
assemble assembled assembling assembly assemblies: 4.2.3 7.3.1
assent assented assenting: 3.2.3 5.1.6 7.3.5
assist assisted assisting assistant assistance: 3.3.1 5.3.4 7.2.1
associate associated associating association: 5.1.2 7.3.1
assure assured assuring assurance: 5.3.4 7.2.1
attach attached attaching attachment: 5.1.6
attempt attempted attempting: 3.3.2 4.4.6 4.6.2 7.1.1
attend attended attending attentive attentively attendance attendant
attention: 3.3.1 4.4.6 4.6.1 5.3.4 7.1.1
audible audience: 4.2.1 4.6.1 5.3.1 7.3.3
automatic automatically: 3.2.2
available availability: 3.3.6 5.3.1 7.1.1
await awaited awaiting: 5.1.5
awful: 4.1.4
awkward: 3.2.2 7.1.1

B
baby babies: 4.1.1
back: 4.3.4
badge: 4.3.3 5.2.5
balcony balconies: 5.2.5
bank: 4.3.4
bargain: 3.3.1
barley: 4.2.3
basic basically: 3.3.6 7.1.1
battery batteries: 4.1.1
bean (=vegetable), been (=past tense of verb 'to be', e.g. 'I have
been . . .'): 7.3.5
bear bore bearing: 5.1.5 7.3.5
beauty beautiful beautifully: 3.3.7 3.3.9 5.2.3 5.4 7.1.1 7.3.2
beg begged begging: 5.1.3 5.4
begin began beginning: 3.1 4.1.1 4.1.2 4.4.6 4.6.2 7.2.2
behave behaved behaving behaviour: 3.2.1 3.2.2 7.3.1

believe believed believing believable belief: 3.1 3.3.4 3.3.5 3.3.6
4.2.1 4.6.1 5.1.1 5.3.1 5.4 7.3.3
beneath: 4.6.2 7.1.1
benefit benefited benefiting beneficial: 3.3.6 4.4.6 5.1.5 7.2.2
berry (=fruit) berries: 5.2.5 7.3.5
berth (e.g. for ship at wharf): 3.2.3
beware: 5.3.2
bicycle bicycles: 3.3.1 4.4.1 4.6.4 5.2.5 7.1.1
birth birthday: 3.2.3 4.6.1 7.1.1
black: 4.3.4
blotch blotches: 4.3.5
blur blurred blurring: 5.1.5
boar (=male swine): 7.3.5
board (=strip of timber/meals and lodging/body of directors):
3.2.3 4.6.3 7.3.5
bond bondage: 5.2.1
bore bored boring boredom: 3.2.3 4.6.3 7.3.1 7.3.5
borrow borrowed borrowing borrower: 4.6.1 7.2.2
boundary boundaries: 4.2.3
box boxes: 5.2.5
bracket bracketed bracketing: 5.1.5
brake (=means of retarding motion): 3.2.4 4.6.3 7.3.5
branch branches: 5.2.5
bread: 4.2.4
break broke broken breakage: 3.2.2 3.2.7 4.4.2 4.6.3 7.3.1 7.3.5
breath: 4.2.4
bridge: 4.3.3 5.2.5
brief: 4.2.1
bright: 4.6.1 4.6.2
brilliance brilliant brilliantly: 4.4.1 4.6.4 7.2.2
bring brought bringing: 4.3.7 7.3.5
Britain: 7.1.1
brush brushes: 5.2.5
bucket: 4.4.4
budge: 4.3.3
budget budgeted budgeting: 5.1.5
bungalow: 4.1.1
burglar: 5.3.2
bury buried burying burial: 4.2.1 7.3.1 7.3.5
bus buses: 3.3.1 4.3.1 5.2.5
business: 3.1 3.2.1 4.6.4 7.1.1
busy busily: 5.2.4
butterfly butterflies: 5.2.5
buy bought buying: 4.3.7 4.6.1 7.3.5
by (=alongside, next): 7.3.5

C

cadge: 4.3.3
cake: 4.4.4
calendar: 5.3.2
call called calling: 3.3.4 3.3.5 4.1.2
campaign: 3.3.1 4.6.2 7.1.1
cancel cancelled cancelling cancellation: 4.4.6 4.4.7 7.1.1 7.2.2
7.3.1
canvas (=cloth used for sails, tents, etc.), canvass (=seek support,
e.g. votes): 3.2.3
care careful carefully: 3.2.2 3.3.6 3.3.9 4.4.4 4.6.2 4.6.4 7.2.2 7.3.2
carry carried carrying carriage: 3.3.1 3.3.4 3.3.5 4.1.1 4.6.1 5.2.2
5.4 7.1.1 7.2.2
casserole: 3.3.1
cassette: 3.3.1
casual casualty casualties: 5.2.1 7.1.1
catalogue: 3.3.1 5.1.1 7.1.1
catastrophe catastrophic: 4.4.1 4.6.4 7.1.1
catarrh: 3.2.1
catch caught catching: 4.3.7 4.6.1
category categories: 3.3.1
cauliflower: 3.3.1
cave: 4.3.9
cease ceased ceasing: 4.4.7
cede (=yield): 3.2.3 (cf. 'seed')
ceiling: 4.2.1 4.6.1 7.3.3
celebrate celebrated celebrating celebration celebrity: 3.3.2 5.1.2
5.4 7.1.1
cellar: 3.3.1
cemetery: 3.2.1 5.3.3 7.1.1
center (U.S.)/centre: 5.3.2
century centuries: 3.3.1 7.1.1
cereal (=edible grain, e.g. breakfast food): 3.2.3 (cf. 'serial')
ceremony ceremonies: 5.2.5
certain certainly: 7.1.1
certificate: 3.2.2 3.3.1 7.1.1
chair chaired chairing: 5.1.5
change changed changing changeable: 3.1 3.2.2 4.1.2 4.3.2 4.6.1
4.6.4 5.1.1
channel: 3.3.1
character: 3.1 3.2.2 7.1.1
chat chatted chatting: 5.1.5 5.1.6
cheat cheated cheating: 5.1.5
cheer cheered cheering cheerful cheerfully: 4.4.1 4.6.4 5.1.5 7.2.2
chief chiefly: 4.2.1 7.3.3
child childhood: 5.2.1

chimney chimneys: 4.2.3 4.6.1 5.2.5
chocolate: 3.1 3.2.2 7.1.1
choose chose choosing choice: 3.3.5 4.4.7 7.2.2
chord (musical term): 3.2.3 7.3.5 (cf. 'cord')
cigarette cigarettes: 5.2.5 7.1.1
circular: 5.3.2 7.1.1
circumstance: 3.3.1 5.3.4 7.1.1
claim claimed claiming claimant: 5.3.4
clean cleaned cleaning: 5.1.3
cleanse cleansed cleansing: 4.4.7
clever cleverly cleverness: 5.2.1
cliff cliffs: 5.2.5
cloak: 4.4.4 4.6.2
clock: 4.4.4
close closed closing closely: 4.4.4
cloth cloths (materials): 4.1.1 7.3.5
clothe clothes (garments): 4.1.1 7.3.5
cluck clucked clucking: 4.4.4
clutch: 4.3.5
clumsy clumsily clumsiness: 3.3.7 7.3.2
coal: 4.4.4
coalesce: 6.2.8
coarse (=rough): 4.6.3 (cf. 'course'): 7.3.5
coincide coincided coinciding coincidence: 6.2.8 7.1.1 7.3.1
collaborate collaborated collaborating collaboration: 3.3.2 6.2.8
    7.2.2
collapse collapsed collapsing collapsible: 4.4.7 5.3.1 6.2.8 7.1.1
    7.3.4
colleague: 6.2.8
collect collected collecting collection collector: 5.1.2 5.3.2 6.2.8
    7.3.1
college: 3.3.1 6.2.8
collide collided colliding collision: 3.3.1 6.2.8 7.1.2
colliery collieries: 5.2.5 7.2.2
comb: 4.1.1
combine combined combining combination: 6.2.8
come came coming: 4.1.1 7.2.2
comfort comfortable: 3.2.2 7.1.2 7.3.2
commence commenced commencing commencement: 3.3.2 4.4.6
    4.4.7 6.2.8 7.3.1
comment: 4.1.1 4.6.1 6.2.8
commit committed committing committee: 4.4.6 5.1.5 6.2.8 7.2.2
common communal community: 6.2.8
communicate communicated communicating communication:
    6.2.8 7.1.2
commute commuted commuting commuter: 5.3.2 5.4

dark darkness: 5.2.1
daughter: 5.3.2
dead: 4.2.4
dealt: 4.2.4 7.1.2
deceive deceived deceiving deceptive deception deceit deceitful
deceitfully: 3.1. 3.2.1 4.2.1 4.4.2 4.4.7 4.6.1 4.6.4 7.3.1 7.3.3
decide decided deciding decisive decisively decision: 3.1 3.2.2 3.3.5
4.1.1 4.4.7 4.6.1 4.6.2 4.6.4
deck: 4.3.4
declare declared declaring declaration: 4.4.7 5.3.2 7.3.1
decline declined declining: 4.4.7 7.2.2
decrease decreased decreasing: 4.4.7
defeat defeated defeating: 5.1.5. 7.1.2
defer deferred deferring: 5.1.5
deficient deficiency: 3.3.6
definite definitely definition: 3.1 3.2.2 3.3.7 3.3.8 4.6.1 7.1.2 7.3.2
defy defied defying defiant defiantly defiance: 5.2.2
delay delayed delaying: 5.2.2
deliberate deliberately: 3.3.6 7.1.2
delicate: 3.3.6
delicious: 3.3.6
deny denied denying denial: 5.2.2
departure: 5.3.2
dependable: 5.3.1
dependant (noun): 3.2.4 5.3.4
dependent (adjective): 3.3.6 5.3.4
describe described describing description: 3.1 3.2.2 4.4.7 4.6.4
5.1.2 7.3.1
desert deserted deserting desertion deserter: 4.6.3 5.3.2 7.2.2
deserve deserved deserving: 4.4.7
design designed designing designer: 3.2.1 3.3.2 5.3.2 5.4 7.1.2
desire desired desiring desirable: 5.3.1
despair despaired despairing: 5.1.5
dessert (= sweet course of meal): 3.2.4
destroy destroyed destroying destroyer destructive destruction:
3.3.4 3.3.5 5.2.2 5.4 7.1.2
deter deterred deterring deterrent deterrence: 5.1.5
determine determined determination: 4.4.7 7.1.2
develop developed developing development: 3.1 3.3.4 3.3.5 4.1.1.
4.1.2 4.4.1 4.4.6 4.6.1 4.6.4 7.1.2
dialogue: 5.1.1
diameter: 5.3.2
differ differed differing different difference: 3.3.6 5.1.5 5.3.4 5.4
7.1.2 7.2.2
difficult difficulty: 3.3.1 4.4.1 4.6.2 4.6.4 5.2.5 7.1.2
digest digested digesting digestible digestion: 5.3.1

145

dine dined dining diner (=a person who dines) dinner (=a meal): 3.3.4 4.1.1 4.1.2 7.3.5
disabled: 6.2.9
disagree disagreed disagreeing disagreeable disagreement: 6.2.9
disappear disappeared disappearing disappearance: 3.1 4.4.2 6.2.9 7.2.2
disappoint disappointed disappointing disappointment: 3.1 3.3.1 4.4.1 4.4.2 4.6.4 5.1.3 5.4 6.2.9 7.3.1
disapprove disapproved disapproving disapproval: 4.4.7 6.2.9 7.3.1
disaster disastrous disastrously: 3.3.1 6.2.9 7.1.3 7.2.2
discharge discharged discharging: 4.4.7
discipline disciplined disciplinary: 5.3.3 7.1.3
discourage discouraged discouraging discouragement: 4.4.7
discreet discreetly discretion: 6.2.9
discriminate discriminated discriminating discrimination: 6.2.9
discuss discussed discussing discussion: 3.3.2 3.3.4 3.3.5 5.1.2 6.2.9 7.1.3
disease diseased: 4.6.1 7.1.3
disgrace disgraceful disgracefully: 6.2.9 7.1.3 7.3.2
disguise disguised disguising: 4.3.2 4.4.7 4.6.1 6.2.9
disgusting: 6.2.9
dishearten disheartened disheartening: 6.2.9
dishonest dishonestly dishonesty: 6.2.9
disinfect disinfected disinfecting disinfectant: 6.2.9
disintegrate disintegrated disintegrating disintegration: 6.2.9 7.1.3
dislike disliked disliking: 6.2.9
dismiss dismissed dismissing dismissal: 6.2.9 7.2.2
disobedient: 6.2.9
disown disowned disowning: 6.2.9
dispense dispensed dispensing dispensary: 5.3.3 6.2.9
disperse dispersed dispersing dispersal: 6.2.9
display displayed displaying: 6.2.9
dispute disputed disputing disputable: 3.3.5 6.2.9
disruptive: 6.2.9
dissatisfy dissatisfied dissatisfying dissatisfaction: 3.1 6.2.9 7.2.2
dissect dissected dissecting dissection: 6.2.9 7.3.1
dissimilar: 6.2.9
dissolve dissolved dissolving: 6.2.9 7.2.2
dissuade dissuaded dissuading: 6.2.9
distance distant: 5.3.4
distillery: 5.3.3
distinguish distinguished distinguishing distinguishable: 6.2.9 7.1.3 7.3.4
distort distorted distorting distortion: 6.2.9
disturb disturbed disturbing disturbance: 5.3.4 6.2.9

divide divided dividing division: 4.4.5 7.3.1 7.3.4
dodge dodged dodging: 4.3.3
draft (=sketch of work to be done, order for drawing money, e.g.
    cheque, etc.): 3.2.3
drag dragged dragging: 4.1.2 4.4.6
draught draughty: 3.2.3 4.3.7 4.6.1 4.6.3
dread dreadful: 4.2.4
dream dreaming: 4.4.2
dress dressed: 5.2.5
drink drank drinking drunk drunkenness: 5.1.6 5.2.1
drudgery: 5.3.3
duly: 4.1.4
dungeon: 5.1.1
durable: 5.3.1
dysentery: 5.3.3.

E
early earlier earliest: 4.2.4 7.1.3
ease easy easily easier easiest: 3.3.7 3.3.8 7.1.3 7.3.2
edge: 4.3.3
eat ate eating edible: 5.3.1 7.3.4
effect effective: 3.2.4 3.3.6 4.6.3
efficient efficiently efficiency: 3.2.1 3.3.6 7.1.3 7.3.2
either: 4.2.1 5.3.2 7.3.3
elect elected electing election: 7.3.4
electric electrical electricity: 4.4.4 7.1.3
elegant elegance: 3.2.2 5.3.4
eligible: 5.3.1
elope eloped eloping: 4.1.1
embarrass embarrassed embarrassing embarrassment: 3.1 3.3.5
    4.4.1 4.6.4 7.2.2
embroider embroidered embroidering embroidery: 5.1.6 5.3.3
emergency emergencies: 3.2.2 4.6.4 7.2.2
emigrate emigrated emigrating emigration emigrant: 5.1.2 7.2.2
eminent eminence: 5.3.4
employ employs employed employing employer: 5.2.2 7.1.3
empty: 4.1.1 4.6.1
enable enabled enabling: 4.4.7 7.2.2
endure endured enduring endurance: 5.3.2 5.3.4
energy: 4.2.3
engage engaged engaging engagement: 3.3.1
enjoy enjoyed enjoying enjoyable enjoyment: 5.2.2 5.4 7.3.4
enter entered entering entrance: 5.1.5 5.3.4 5.4 7.1.3 7.2.2
entice enticed enticing: 4.4.7
entire entirely entirety: 3.3.6 3.3.7 3.3.8 7.3.2

equal equalled equalling equally equality: 4.4.6 4.4.7 5.2.1 7.2.2
equip equipped equipping equipment: 3.3.1 3.3.4 3.3.5 4.4.6 7.1.3
especially: 4.4.5 4.6.2 5.2.4 7.1.3
everyone: 7.1.3
everything: 3.1 3.2.2
exact exactly: 4.6.1 5.2.4
exaggerate exaggerated exaggerating exaggeration: 3.1 3.3.5 4.4.1
    4.6.4 5.1.2 5.4 7.2.3
examine examined examining examination: 5.1.2 5.4
exceed exceeded exceeding excess excessive: 4.2.2 7.3.1
excellent excellently excellence: 3.3.6 4.6.1 7.1.3
except exception: 4.6.1
excite excited exciting excitable excitement: 4.6.1 5.1.1 5.3.1 5.4
    7.1.3
exclude excluded excluding exclusion exclusive exclusively: 5.1.2
excuse excused excusing: 4.6.1 7.3.4
exercise: 7.1.3
exist existed existing existence: 3.1 5.3.4
expel expelled expelling expulsion: 4.4.6 4.4.7 5.1.4
expense expensive: 7.1.3
experience experienced experiencing: 3.1 3.2.2 4.4.1 4.6.4 5.3.4
    7.1.3
explain explained explaining explanation explanatory explicable:
    4.4.7 5.3.3 7.2.3
explore explored exploring exploration: 4.4.7 5.3.2
express expressed expressing expressive expression: 5.1.2 5.4
extend extended extending extensive extensively extension extent:
    3.3.6 7.3.2
extravagant extravagance: 7.1.3

F
factory factories: 5.2.5 5.3.3 5.4
fail failed failing failure: 5.3.2 7.2.3
faithful faithfully: 4.6.2 5.2.3 5.4 7.1.3 7.3.2
familiar: 5.3.2
fascinate fascinated fascinating fascination: 3.3.5 4.4.7 5.1.2 5.4
    7.1.3
fashion fashionable: 4.6.1 7.1.3
fasten fastened fastening: 4.6.1
fatal fatality: 5.2.1
fatigue: 5.1.1
favo(u)rite: 3.2.2 7.1.3 (no u in US)
fear feared fearing: 5.1.5 7.2.3
feature: 5.3.2 7.1.3
February: 4.4.1 4.6.4 7.1.3

feel felt feeling: 5.1.4
fellow fellowship: 5.2.1
female feminine: 4.1.1. 4.6.1 7.1.3
ferry ferries: 5.2.5
festival festive festivity: 4.4.2 5.2.1
fetch fetched fetching: 4.3.5
fiction fictitious: 3.2.2 7.1.3
fidget fidgeted fidgeting: 4.6.1 5.1.5 7.2.3
field: 4.2.1 4.6.1
fiend: 4.2.1
fight fought fighting: 4.3.7 4.6.1
fillet filleted filleting: 5.1.5
film: 4.4.1
filter filtered filtering: 5.1.5
final finally: 4.6.1 5.2.4 5.4 7.2.3
finance financial: 4.4.5 4.6.1 7.1.3
find found finding: 4.1.1
fit fitted fitting: 4.4.6 5.1.5 5.4
five: 4.3.9
flatter flattered flattering flattery flatterer: 5.3.2 7.2.3
flexible: 5.3.1
float floated floating: 4.1.1 5.1.5
fluorescent fluorescence: 5.3.4 7.1.3
follow followed following: 4.6.1
force forced forcing forceful forcefully forcible: 5.1.3 5.2.4 5.3.1
foreign foreigner: 3.2.1 4.2.1 7.1.3 7.3.3
forfeit forfeited forfeiting: 4.2.1 7.3.3
forget forgot forgetting forgotten forgetful forgetfulness: 4.4.2
    7.2.3
formidable: 5.3.1
fortnight: 3.3.1 4.6.1
fortunate fortunately fortune: 3.3.7 3.3.8 4.4.1 4.6.3 7.1.3 7.3.2
foul fouled fouling: 5.1.4
fourth: 4.6.1
fragrant fragrance: 5.3.4
frantic frantically: 4.4.4
fraught: 4.3.7
freight: 3.2.1 4.6.4
frequent frequently: 3.3.6 7.1.3
fridge: 4.3.3
friend friendly friendliness friendship: 3.1 3.2.2 4.6.1 4.6.2 7.1.3
fright frightened frightening frightful: 3.2.2 4.3.7 4.6.1 7.1.3 7.3.1
fry fried frying: 4.1.1 5.2.2
fulfil fulfilled fulfilling fulfilment: 3.3.4 5.1.4 7.2.3
full fully: 5.2.4
fun funny funnily: 4.2.3 5.2.4 7.3.2

furious furiously fury: 3.1 4.4.1 4.6.4 7.1.3
furniture: 5.3.2 7.1.3
further: 5.3.2

G
gait (=manner of walking): 3.2.3
gallery galleries: 5.3.3
gallop galloped galloping: 4.4.2 4.4.6 7.2.3
garage: 4.6.1 7.1.3
gas: 4.3.1
gate: 3.2.3 (cf. gait)
gauge: 3.3.1 7.1.3
general generally: 5.2.4 7.1.3
generous: 4.3.2 7.1.3
genius geniuses: 4.3.2 5.2.5
gentle: 3.3.6 4.3.2
genuine: 4.3.2
get got getting: 3.3.5
gist: 4.3.2
give gave giving: 4.3.9
glacier: 4.1.1
glimpse glimpsed glimpsing: 4.4.6 4.4.7
glove gloves: 4.3.9
gorgeous: 5.1.1
gorilla (species of ape): 7.3.5 (cf. 'guerilla')
government: 3.1 4.4.1 4.6.4 7.1.4
grace gracious graciously: 4.4.5 5.1.1 7.1.4 7.3.2
gradual gradually: 5.2.4 5.4
grateful gratefully gratitude: 3.3.6 7.3.2
grater (=utensil for grating)/greater (=larger, etc.): 3.2.3
greed greedy greedily greediness: 5.2.4
greet greeted greeting: 4.1.2 5.1.5 7.2.3
grievous grievously: 5.2.4 5.4
grit gritted gritting: 4.1.2
groan (=sound)/grown (=increased in size): 7.3.5
grocery groceries: 5.2.5 5.4
grumble grumbled grumbling: 4.4.7
guarantee: 3.3.1 4.3.2 4.6.1 5.2.5 7.1.4
guess guessed guessing: 4.3.2 7.2.3
guerilla (e.g. warfare): 7.3.5
guest: 4.3.2 4.6.1
guilt guilty guiltily: 4.3.2 7.1.4 7.3.2
guitar: 4.3.2

H

I

ignore ignored ignoring ignorant ignorance: 5.3.4 5.4
illegal: 6.2.1 6.2.2 7.2.3
illegible: 6.2.6
illogical: 6.2.2
illustrate illustrated illustrating illustration: 5.1.2 7.2.3
imagine imagined imagining imaginative imaginable imaginary
    imagination: 5.1.1 5.3.1 5.3.3 6.2.7 7.1.4
imitate imitated imitating imitation: 5.1.2 7.2.3
immaculate: 6.2.4
immaterial: 6.2.2
immature: 6.2.5
immediate immediately: 3.1 3.3.7 3.3.8 4.4.1 4.6.4 6.2.4 7.1.4
immense immensely: 3.3.6 6.2.5
imminent: 6.2.7 7.2.3
immoral: 6.2.2
immortal: 6.2.2
immovable: 6.2.1 6.2.6
immunis(z)e: 6.2.5
impact: 6.2.7
impartial: 6.2.2
impatient impatiently impatience: 4.4.1 4.4.5 4.6.4 6.2.3 7.1.4
impeccable: 6.2.6
imperceptible imperceptibly: 6.2.6
imperfect imperfection: 6.2.1 6.2.5
impetuous: 6.2.7
implement: 6.2.7
implicate implicated implicating implication: 6.2.7
impolite: 6.2.1 6.2.4
important importance: 3.3.6 5.3.4 5.4
impossible: 5.3.1 6.2.1 7.2.3
impracticable: 6.2.6
impress impressed impressing impressive impression: 6.2.7
improbable: 6.2.1
improve improved improving improvement: 6.2.7
impudent impudence: 6.2.3
impulse impulsive: 6.2.7
inaccessible: 5.3.1
inaccurate: 4.6.1 6.2.1
inadequate inadequately inadequacy: 3.3.7 7.3.2
inattentive: 6.2.5
incensed: 6.2.7
incident incidentally: 5.3.4 5.4 6.2.7 7.1.4
incision: 6.2.7
include included including inclusive inclusion: 5.1.2
incoherent: 6.2.3
incomparable: 6.2.6

lodge lodged lodging: 4.3.3
lonely loneliness. 5.2.1 7.1.4
look looked looking: 4.4.4
loose (not tight): 3.2.5 3.2.6 3.3.6
lorry lorries: 5.2.5 5.4
lose lost losing: 3.2.6 3.2.7 7.2.3
love loved loving: 4.3.9
loyal loyalty: 5.2.1
luck lucky luckily: 4.3.4 4.4.4
luxuriant luxuriance luxury: 5.3.4 7.1.4

M
machine machinery: 7.1.4
magistrate: 4.1.1 4.6.1
magnificent magnificence: 5.3.4 5.4 7.1.4
maintain maintained maintaining maintenance: 3.1 3.2.2 4.4.1
    4.6.4 7.1.4
make made making: 4.1.2 4.4.4 5.1.6
manage managed managing manageable management manager:
    4.6.1 5.1.1 5.4 7.1.4
manicure: 5.3.2
manner (=way thing is done or happens)/manor (=large house
    with estate from feudal period): 3.2.3
manoeuvre manoeuvred manoeuvring: 3.2.2 7.1.4
mansion: 4.4.5
manual: 3.3.6
manufacture manufactured manufacturing manufacturer: 5.1.6
    5.3.2 7.1.4
marry married marrying marriage: 3.3.4 3.3.5 4.1.1 4.6.1
marvel marvelled marvelling: 5.1.4
mask: 4.1.2
material: 4.6.1 7.1.5
meadow: 4.2.4
mean meant meaning: 4.2.4
measure measured measuring measurement: 4.6.1 7.1.5
mechanical: 3.3.6 7.1.5
medicine: 3.2.2 7.1.5
Mediterranean: 3.2.2 7.1.5
meat (=animal flesh for food)/meet (verb): 7.3.5
meet met meeting: 5.1.5 7.2.3
memorable: 5.3.1
mend mended mending: 4.1.1 7.2.3
mercy merciful mercifully: 5.2.3
mere merely: 5.2.4
merry merrier merriest merrily merriment: 5.2.1 5.2.2

might: 4.3.7 4.6.2
migrate migrated migrating migration migratory: 5.3.3
military: 5.3.3
millinery: 5.3.3
mimic mimicked mimicking: 5.1.1
miner (=person who mines)/minor (=lesser, junior, etc.): 3.2.3
miniature: 3.2.2 7.1.5
minute minutes: 3.3.1
miscellany miscellaneous: 3.1 4.1.1 4.4.1 4.6.1 4.6.4 7.1.5
mischief mischievous: 3.3.6 4.2.1 4.6.1 7.1.5 7.3.3
miss missed missing: 7.3.5
mist (=light fog): 7.3.5
moan (=lament, complain)/mown (past tense of 'mow'): 3.2.3
modern: 4.4.1
moisture: 5.3.2
moment: 4.1.1 4.6.2
monastery: 5.3.3
money: 4.2.3
monkey: 4.2.3
moor moored mooring: 5.1.5
mop: 4.1.1
morale: 3.2.4
mortal mortally: 5.2.4
mountain: 4.4.2 7.1.5
mown (past tense of 'mow'): 3.2.3 (cf. 'moan')
much: 4.3.5
muscle muscles muscular/mussel (mollusc, sea food): 3.2.3 4.6.3
musician: 4.4.5
mystery mysterious mysteriously: 5.2.4 5.4 7.1.5 7.3.2

N
narrowly: 4.6.1
national: 4.4.5
natural naturally: 4.6.1 5.2.4 7.1.5
necessary necessarily necessity necessities: 3.1 3.2.2 3.3.7 3.3.8 3.3.9
    4.1.1 4.4.1 4.6.1 4.6.4 7.1.5 7.3.2
necklace: 4.6.2
negligible: 5.3.1
negotiate negotiated negotiating negotiable negotiation: 4.6.1
    5.3.2 5.4
neighbour: 4.2.1 4.6.1 7.1.5
neither: 4.2.1 7.3.3
net netted netting: 5.1.5
new (=opposite of 'old'): 3.2.5 3.2.6 (cf. 'knew')
newspaper: 3.3.1

nil: 4.3.1
ninth: 4.1.4
no (=opposite of 'yes'): 3.2.5 3.2.6 (cf. 'know')
nonsense nonsensical: 3.2.2
notice noticed noticing notices noticeable: 3.3.4 3.3.5 4.1.1 5.1.1
    5.1.3 5.1.6 5.2.5 5.3.1 5.4 7.1.5
novel novelty: 5.2.1
now (=at this moment): 3.2.6
numerous: 7.1.5
nursery: 5.3.3

O
obey obeyed obeying obedient obediently obedience: 4.2.3 5.3.4
    5.4 7.1.5 7.3.1
object objected objecting objectionable objection: 5.1.2
observe observed observing observant observer observation: 5.3.4
obsolescent obsolescence: 5.3.4
obvious: 5.4 7.1.5
occasion occasional occasionally: 3.1 3.3.1 3.3.7 3.3.8 4.4.1 4.6.2
    4.6.4 7.2.4 7.3.2
occupy occupied occupying occupier occupant occupation: 7.2.4
    7.3.1
occur occurred occurring occurrence: 3.1 3.3.4 3.3.5 4.1.1 4.4.6
    4.6.1 5.1.5 7.3.1
offend offended offending offensive offence: 5.3.4
offer offered offering: 5.1.5
officer: 3.3.1 7.2.4
of (=possessive): 3.2.5 7.3.5
off (=not on): 3.2.5 3.2.7 7.3.5
omit omitted omitting omission: 3.3.4 3.3.5 5.1.3 5.1.5
open opened opening: 4.1.1 4.1.2 4.4.6 4.6.1 7.2.4
operate operated operating operation operator: 3.3.1 3.3.2 4.4.5
    4.6.2 5.3.2 5.4 7.3.1
opinion: 4.4.1 4.6.1
opponent: 4.6.1
opportunity opportunities: 3.1 4.4.1 4.6.2 4.6.4 5.2.5 7.2.4
oppose opposed opposing opposite opposition: 4.4.7 4.6.2
order ordered ordering: 5.1.5
organis(z)e organis(z)ed organis(z)ing organis(z)er organis(z)ation:
    5.3.2
origin original originally: 3.3.7 5.2.4 7.1.5 7.3.2
ought: 4.3.7
outrageous: 5.1.1
outwit outwitted outwitting: 5.1.5
own owned owning owner ownership: 5.2.1

oxygen: 3.3.1 7.1.5

P

pack packed packing: 4.4.4
pail (=bucket): 3.2.3 (cf. 'pale')
pain painful painfully: 3.2.3 5.2.3
pair paired pairing: 3.2.3 5.1.5
palace palatial: 4.4.5
pale (=faintly coloured): 3.2.3 (cf. 'pail')
pancake: 4.1.1
pane (e.g. of glass): 3.2.3 (cf. 'pain')
panic panicked panicking: 5.1.1
parallel: 3.1 7.2.4
pare (=trim): 3.2.3 (cf. 'pair')
parent parenthood: 5.2.1
particular particularly: 3.3.6 3.3.7 3.3.8 5.3.2 7.1.5
pass passed passing passage: 3.2.7 3.3.5 7.3.5
passenger: 4.6.1 7.2.4
passionate: 4.4.5
past: 3.2.4 7.3.5
patch patches: 4.3.5 5.2.5
patient patience: 3.3.6 5.3.4 5.4
patriot patriotic patriotism: 5.2.1
patrol patrolled patrolling: 4.4.6 5.1.4 5.4 7.2.4
pause (=break): 3.2.3
paws (=plural of 'paw'): 3.2.3
peace peaceful peacefully peaceable: 3.2.2 3.3.9 5.1.1 5.2.3 7.1.5
   7.3.5
peak (=summit): 3.2.3 (cf. 'pique')
peculiar peculiarly: 5.3.2 7.1.5
pedal pedalled pedalling pedals: 5.1.4 5.2.5
peer peered peering: 3.2.3 (cf. 'pier')
penitent penitence: 5.3.4
pension: 3.2.2
people: 7.1.5
perceive perceived perceiving perceptive perceptible perception:
   3.3.2 4.2.1 5.1.3 7.3.1 7.3.4
perform performed performing performer performance
   performances: 3.3.1 5.2.5 7.1.5
perilous perilously: 5.2.4
permanent permanence: 5.3.4
permit permitted permitting permissible permission: 4.4.5 5.1.5
   5.3.1 7.2.4 7.3.1 7.3.4
persevere persevered persevering perseverance: 3.3.5 5.1.3 7.1.5
   7.3.1

159

persistent persistence: 3.3.6
personal: 7.2.4
personnel: 3.2.4
persuade persuading persuasive persuasion: 3.2.2 4.4.7 4.6.4 5.1.2
5.1.3 5.4 7.1.5
pick picked picking: 4.4.4
picnic picnicked picnicking: 5.1.1 7.1.5
pie: 4.2.1
piece pieces: 4.2.1 5.2.5 7.3.5
pier (=support of spans of bridge, structure running out to sea):
3.2.3 (cf. 'peer')
pierce pierced piercing: 4.2.1 5.1.6
pigeon: 5.1.1
pilfer pilfered pilfering: 5.1.5
pillar: 5.3.2
pilot piloted piloting: 5.1.5
pipe piped piping: 4.1.2
pique (=wounded pride): 3.2.3 (cf. 'peak')
pitch pitches: 4.3.5
pity pitied pitiful pitifully: 5.2.3
pivot pivoted pivoting: 5.1.5
plane planed planing/plan planned planning: 4.1.2
plausible: 5.3.1
play played playing playful playfully: 5.1.6 5.2.2 5.2.3
please pleased pleasing pleasant pleasure pleasurable: 3.1 4.2.4
7.3.1
plum (=fruit)/plumb (=measure depth, work as plumber, etc.):
3.2.3
plus: 4.3.1
pocket: 4.4.4 7.1.5
poison poisoned poisoning poisonous: 3.3.1 3.3.6
poke poked poking: 4.4.4
popular popularity: 5.3.2 7.1.5
portable: 5.3.1
possess possessed possessing possession: 3.1 3.3.5 3.4.3 7.2.4 7.3.1
possible possibility: 5.3.1 7.1.5
postpone postponed postponing postponement: 5.1.6
potato potatoes: 5.2.5
pottery: 5.3.3
practice (noun): 3.2.7 4.4.7 7.3.5
practicable: 5.3.1 7.3.4
practise practised practising: 3.2.4 3.3.2 7.2.4 7.3.1 7.3.5
pray prayed praying prayer: 3.2.3 5.1.3
precede preceded preceding precedent precedence: 3.3.2 4.2.2
5.3.4
precious: 3.2.1 4.6.1 7.1.5

precise precisely precision: 3.3.7 3.3.8
prefer preferred preferring preferable preferably preference: 3.3.4
3.3.5 4.4.6 5.1.5 5.4 7.2.4 7.3.1
prehistoric: 4.1.1 7.1.5
prepare prepared preparing preparatory preparation: 5.1.2 5.3.3
5.4 7.1.5
present presence: 4.6.1 5.3.4
pressure: 4.6.1 5.3.2 7.2.4
pretend pretended pretending pretence: 5.3.4
prevail prevailed prevailing: 5.1.4
previously: 3.3.6 7.1.5
prey: 4.2.3
priest: 4.2.1
primary primarily: 3.3.6 5.3.3
principal principally: 3.2.4 3.3.1 3.3.7 4.6.3 7.1.5 7.3.5
principle (=fundamental truth, moral law): 7.3.5
prise (=force open by leverage)/prize (=reward): 3.2.3
privacy private privately: 3.3.9
privilege privileged: 3.2.2 4.6.4 7.1.5
probable probably: 5.3.1 7.1.5
proceed proceeded proceeding procedure: 3.2.2 3.3.2 4.2.2 4.4.2
7.1.5
produce produced producing productive production producer:
5.3.2 7.1.5 7.3.1
profit profited profiting: 5.1.5
progress progressed progressing progressive progression: 7.2.4
7.3.1
prominent prominence: 5.3.4
promise promised promising: 4.4.7 5.1.6
prompt promptly: 3.3.6
pronounce pronounced pronouncing pronunciation
pronounceable: 5.1.1
propose proposed proposing proposal: 7.2.4
prosecute prosecuted prosecuting prosecution: 7.3.2
prospector: 5.3.2
prosper prospered prospering prosperity: 5.2.1 7.2.4
psychology psychological psychologist: 3.1 4.4.1 4.6.4 7.1.5
pulley: 4.2.3
puny: 4.1.1
pure purity: 5.2.1
purpose: 7.1.5
purvey purveyed purveying: 4.2.3

Q
quack: 4.3.6

quaint: 4.3.6
quake: 4.3.6
quantity quantities: 4.3.6 5.2.5
quarrel quarrelled quarrelling: 4.3.6 4.4.6 4.4.7 5.1.4 5.4 7.1.5
quarry: 4.3.6
quarter: 4.3.6
quartet: 4.3.6
quash: 4.3.6
quay: 4.3.6
queen: 4.6.2
query queries: 5.2.5
queue: 3.1 3.2.4 3.3.1 4.3.6 7.1.5
question: 4.3.6 4.6.1 7.1.5
quick quickly: 3.3.6 4.3.6 7.1.5
quiet quietly: 3.2.5 3.2.6 3.2.7 3.3.9 4.3.6 4.6.1 5.2.4 7.3.5
quit quitted quitting: 5.1.5
quite: 3.2.6 4.3.6 7.3.5

R
radical radically: 3.3.6 7.1.5
radio radios: 5.2.5
rake raked raking: 4.4.4
rain rainy 3.2.3 (cf. 'reign', 'rein')
react reacted reacting reaction: 4.4.4 7.1.5
ready readily readiness: 4.2.3 4.6.1 5.2.1 5.4 7.1.5
real really reality: 3.3.9 4.6.2 5.2.1 5.2.4 7.1.5
realis(z)e realis(z)ed realis(z)ing: 3.1 3.3.2 4.4.1 4.6.4 7.2.4
reason reasoned reasoning reasonable reasonably: 3.3.7 3.3.8 7.1.5
receive received receiving receipt receptive reception: 3.1 3.3.2
    3.3.4 3.3.5 4.2.1 4.4.7 7.3.1 7.3.3
recent recently: 3.3.6 7.1.6
recognis(z)e recognis(z)ed recognis(z)ing recognis(z)able recogni-
    tion 3.1 4.4.7 5.1.1 5.3.1 5.4 7.1.6 7.3.1 7.3.4
recommend recommended recommending recommendation:
    3.2.2 7.1.6
recruit recruited recruiting: 5.1.5
recuperate recuperated recuperating recuperation: 4.1.1
recur recurred recurring recurrent recurrence: 5.1.5 7.3.1
refer referred referring reference: 3.2.2 4.4.6 4.6.4 5.1.5 7.3.1
reflection: 7.1.5
refrigerator: 3.3.1
refuse refused refusing refusal: 4.6.2
register: 5.3.2
regret regretted regretting regretful regretfully regrettable
    regrettably: 3.2.2 3.3.5 5.1.5 5.3.1 5.4 7.3.4

regular regularly: 5.3.2 7.1.6
regulation: 3.2.2 4.6.4
reign (=sovereignty): 3.2.3 4.1.1 7.3.3
rein (=long narrow strap used to control horse, etc.): 3.2.3 (cf. 'rain')
rejoice rejoiced rejoicing: 4.6.2 7.1.6
relative relatively relation: 3.2.2 4.6.4 7.1.6
release released releasing: 5.1.6
religious: 4.6.1 7.1.6
reluctant reluctantly reluctance: 4.4.2 7.1.6 7.3.2
rely relied relying reliable reliance: 5.2.2 5.3.1 7.3.4
remember remembered remembering remembrance: 4.4.2 5.3.2 7.1.6 7.3.1
render rendered rendering: 5.1.5
repeal repealed repealing: 4.4.6
repeat repeated repeating repetitive repetition: 3.3.2 5.1.5 7.1.6
repentant repentance: 5.3.4
replace replaced replacing replacement: 7.3.1
request: 4.6.2
require required requiring: 5.3.2 5.4
rescue rescued rescuing: 4.6.1
resemble resembled resembling resemblance: 5.1.6
reside resided residing resident residence: 5.3.4 7.3.1
resist resisted resisting resistant resistance resistible: 5.3.1 5.3.4 7.1.6
respectful respectfully respectable: 5.2.3 5.3.1 7.1.6
responsible responsibly responsibility responsibilities: 3.1 3.2.2 3.3.7 4.4.1 4.6.4 5.3.1 5.4 7.1.6
reunite reunited reuniting reunion: 4.4.2
reveal revealed revealing: 5.1.4
reverent reverence: 5.3.4
rhythm: 3.1 7.1.6
rich: 4.3.5
right (=opposite of wrong): 3.2.5 3.2.6 3.3.6 (cf. 'write'): 7.3.5
ring rang ringing: 3.2.3 (also=circlet of gold worn on finger, etc., and cf. 'wring')
rivet riveted riveting: 5.1.5
rob robbed robbing robbery: 7.3.1
rock: 4.3.4
rogue: 3.2.2
rot rotted rotting rotten: 3.3.6 5.1.5
rough: 3.2.7 4.6.3
run ran running: 3.3.4 3.3.5 4.4.6

S
sack: 4.3.4
safe safely safety: 3.3.7 3.3.9 4.6.2 5.2.4 5.4 7.3.2
sail (=piece of canvas stretched on rigging of ship)/sale (=selling):
    3.2.3 3.2.4
same: 4.6.2
satisfy satisfied satisfying satisfactory satisfactorily satisfaction:
    3.3.5 3.3.7 3.3.8 3.3.9 5.13 5.3.3 5.4 7.1.6
say said saying: 4.1.1
scarce scarcely scarcity: 3.3.7 7.1.6
schedule: 3.3.1
science scientific scientifically scientist: 4.6.1 7.1.6
scissors: 3.3.1 7.2.4
scorn scornful scornfully: 5.2.3
seam (=line of junction of two edges, e.g. of cloth sewn
    together)/seem (=appear to be): 3.2.3
search searching. 4.2.4
secondary: 5.3.3
secretary secretaries: 5.3.3 5.4 7.1.6
secure securely security: 5.3.2 7.1.6
seed (e.g. of fruit, vegetable): 3.2.3 (cf. 'cede')
seem seemed seeming: 3.2.3 (cf. 'seam')
seize seized seizing seizure: 3.3.2 4.2.1 7.3.3
sensible: 5.3.1 7.1.6
sensitive: 3.3.6
sentence: 4.6.1
separate separated separating separately separation: 3.1 3.2.2 3.3.7
    3.3.8 5.1.3 7.1.6 7.3.1 7.3.2
sequence: 3.2.2 7.1.6
sergeant: 5.1.1
serial (=series): 3.2.3 4.6.3 (cf. 'cereal')
serve served serving service serviced servicing serviceable: 5.1.1
    5.2.1 5.3.1 5.4
severe severely: 5.3.2 7.1.6
shame shameful shamefully: 5.2.3
sheer: 3.2.4
shelf shelves: 5.2.5
shield shielded shielding: 4.1.2 4.2.1
shine shone shining. 3.3.4 4.1.1
shop shopped shopping: 3.3.5 4.1.2
shovel shovelled shovelling: 5.1.4
shrink shrank shrinking shrinkage: 5.2.1
siege. 4.2.1
sign: 4.1.1
signal signalled signalling: 5.1.4 7.2.4
silent silently silence: 4.4.2 7.1.6

silhouette: 3.2.2 7.1.6
similar similarly similarity: 3.1 7.2.4 7.3.2
simplify simplified simplifying simplification: 5.2.2
sincere sincerely sincerity: 3.3.7 3.3.9 5.2.4 5.4 7.3.2
skill skilled skilful skilfully: 3.3.6 7.2.4 7.3.2
slaughter: 5.3.2
smock (=loose-fitting shirt-like garment): 4.1.1 4.4.4
smoke smoked smoking: 4.1.1 4.4.4
soar soared soaring: 3.2.3 (cf. 'sore')
social socially society sociable: 4.1.1 4.2.1 4.6.1 5.3.1 7.2.4 7.3.2
socket: 4.4.4
soldier: 4.1.1 4.6.1
solemn: 4.1.1 4.6.1
some something: 3.2.3 4.6.1 (cf. 'sum')
sore (=painful): 3.2.3 (cf. 'soar')
sort (=type)/sought (past tense of 'seek'): 3.2.3
sovereign: 4.2.1
space spacious: 4.4.5 5.1.1 5.4 7.1.6
sparkle sparkled sparkling: 5.1.6
speak spoke speaking speaker speech: 4.1.2 4.6.1
special specially speciality specialities: 3.3.6 3.3.7 4.4.5 5.2.1
spectacular: 5.3.2 7.1.6
speed speedometer speedily speedy: 4.2.2 5.2.4 5.3.2
spill spilled spilling spilt: 4.1.2
spit spat spitting: 4.1.2
spoil spoiled spoiling spoilt: 4.1.2 7.2.4
spread: 4.2.4
spy spied spying: 4.1.1
stake (pointed post for driving into ground): 3.2.3 (cf. 'steak')
stare stared staring: 3.2.4 4.1.1
star starred starring: 5.1.5
station: 3.3.1
stationary (=not moving): 3.2.4 4.6.3 5.3.3
stationery (=writing materials): 5.3.3
steady steadily steadier steadiest steadiness: 4.2.4 5.2.2 7.1.6
steak (=thick slice of beef, etc.): 3.2.3 (cf. 'stake')
steal stole stealing: 4.6.2 7.2.4
stick stuck sticking: 4.1.2
stir stirred stirring: 5.1.5
stomach: 3.2.1 7.1.6
stop stopped stopping: 3.3.4 3.3.5 4.1.2
storey storeys (=a floor of a building): 3.2.3 5.2.5
story stories (=tale): 3.2.3 5.2.5
straight: 3.2.2 4.4.1 4.6.4
strength strengthen strengthened strengthening: 3.2.2 4.6.4 7.1.6
strike struck striking: 4.4.4

strip stripped stripping (cf. stripe striped striping): 4.1.2
struggle struggled struggling: 5.1.3 5.4 7.1.6
strut strutted strutting: 5.1.5
student: 3.3.1
study studies studying: 5.2.2
stumble stumbles stumbling: 4.4.7
stupid stupidity: 4.1.1 5.2.1
submit submitted submitting: 5.1.5
subsidiary: 5.3.3
succeed succeeded succeeding success successful successfully: 3.1
   3.3.1 3.3.7 3.3.8 3.3.9 4.2.2 4.4.1 4.6.1 4.6.2 4.6.4 7.2.4 7.3.1
   7.3.2
such: 4.3.5
sudden suddenly suddenness: 5.2.1 5.4 7.2.4
suffer suffered suffering: 5.1.5 5.4
suffice sufficed sufficient: 5.3.4 7.1.6
suggest suggested suggesting suggestion: 3.3.2 5.1.2 5.1.6 5.4 7.1.6
   7.3.1
suit suited suiting suitable suitability: 5.1.5 5.2.1
sum (=total): 3.2.3 (cf. 'some')
sunshine: 4.6.2
super/supper (=meal): 4.1.2
supersede superseded superseding: 4.2.2
supervise supervised supervising supervisor supervision: 5.3.2
surface: 7.1.6
surgery: 5.3.3 7.1.6
surprise surprised surprising: 3.1 3.3.5 4.6.1 7.1.6
surrender surrendered surrendering: 5.1.3 5.4
survey surveyed surveying surveyor: 4.2.3 5.2.2
Surrey: 4.2.3
sweat: 4.2.4
sword: 4.6.2
system systematic systematically: 4.4.1 7.1.6

T
tackle tackled tackling: 4.4.7
take took taking: 4.1.2
tangible: 5.3.1
tar tarred tarring: 5.1.5
teach taught teaching teacher: 4.3.7
tear tore tearing: 5.1.5
telephone telephoned telephoning telephonist: 5.1.6 7.1.6
tell told telling: 4.1.2
temperature: 3.3.1 7.1.6
tempt tempted tempting temptation: 4.1.2

true truly truth truthful truthfully: 3.1 3.3.6 3.3.7 4.1.4 5.2.3 5.2.4
5.4 7.3.2
trumpet trumpeted trumpeting trumpeter: 5.1.5 5.3.2
try tried trying: 4.1.1 4.6.2 5.1.3 5.2.2
tug tugged tugging. 4.1.2
tune tuned tuning tuneful tunefully: 4.1.1 4.1.2
turkey turkeys: 4.2.3 5.2.5
two (=number): 3.2.5 3.2.6

U
ugly ugliness: 4.1.1
umbrella: 3.1 4.4.1 4.6.4 7.2.4
umpire: 5.3.2
uncertain: 6.2.1
uncoil uncoiled uncoiling: 5.1.4
undecided: 6.2.1
undoubtedly: 3.2.2
unite united uniting: 5.1.6
unnecessary unnecessarily: 4.4.1 7.2.4
unselfish unselfishly: 6.2.1
until: 3.1
unveil unveiled unveiling: 5.1.4
urge urged urging: 4.1.2
us: 4.3.1
usual usually: 3.1 3.3.6 4.4.1 4.6.1 4.6.2 4.6.4 7.1.6
use used using useful usefully usable: 5.2.3 5.3.1 7.2.4

V
vacuum: 4.1.1 4.6.1
vague: 5.1.1
valley valleys: 4.2.3 5.2.5 5.4 7.2.4
vary varied varying variable various variously variety: 5.2.1 5.4
7.3.2 7.3.4
vegetable: 3.2.1 7.1.6
veil veiled veiling: 5.1.3 7.3.3
vengeance: 5.1.1
ventilate ventilated ventilating ventilation: 5.1.2
vessel: 4.6.1
veterinary: 5.3.3 7.1.6
vicious: 3.2.1 4.6.4
view viewed viewing viewer: 4.1.2 4.6.1
vigilant vigilance: 5.3.4
village villager: 3.3.1 7.1.6

vinegar: 5.3.2
violent violently violence: 3.2.2 5.3.4 5.4 7.1.6
visible: 5.3.1 7.1.6
visit visited visiting visitor: 4.4.6 5.1.3 5.1.5 5.3.2 5.4 7.1.6
volley: 4.2.3
vulgar: 5.3.2

W

waist (=middle): 7.3.5 (cf. 'waste')
wait waited waiting: 3.2.3 (cf. 'weight'): 4.1.2 4.6.1 5.1.5
waive (=forgo)/wave (=move to and fro, e.g. hands, motion of sea, etc.): 3.2.3
wallet: 4.3.8
wallow: 4.3.8
wander: 4.3.8
warrior: 4.3.8
wash washed washing: 4.3.8
wasp: 4.3.8
waste (=useless): 3.2.4 4.6.3 7.3.5 (cf. 'waist')
watch watched watching: 4.3.8
weak weakness (=frail): 3.2.3 (cf. 'week')
weapon: 4.2.4
wear wore wearing: 3.2.6
we're (=we are)/were (past tense of 'to be'—'we were/you were'): 3.2.5 3.2.6 3.2.7 7.3.5
weary wearied wearily wearier weariest weariness: 4.2.3 5.2.1 5.2.2 5.4 7.1.6
weather (rain, etc.): 3.2.5 3.2.6 7.3.5 (cf. 'whether')
Wednesday: 3.1 3.2.1 4.6.4
week (=seven days): 3.2.3 (cf. 'weak')
weigh weighed weighing weight (amount thing, etc., weighs, heaviness): 3.2.3 4.1.1 4.2.1 4.6.1 (cf. 'wait')
weird: 4.2.1 4.6.1 7.3.3
welcome: 4.4.3
welfare: 4.4.3
well: 4.4.3
wheel wheeled wheeling: 5.1.4
where (place, position): 3.2.5 3.2.6 3.2.7 7.3.5 (cf. 'were')
whether (=if): 3.2.6 7.3.5 (cf. 'weather')
which: 4.3.5
whirr whirred whirring: 5.1.5
wholly: 4.1.4
who's (=who is)/whose (possessive): 3.2.5 3.2.6
wicked: 4.4.4

wife wives: 5.2.5
win won winning: 4.1.2
wish wishes wished wishing: 5.2.5
wool woollen: 3.1 7.2.4
world: 4.3.8
worry worried worrying worrier: 4.1.1 4.6.1 5.2.2
worse: 4.3.8
worship: 4.3.8
worthless: 4.3.8
wriggle wriggled wriggling: 4.4.7 7.2.4
wring (=press, squeeze, twist): 3.2.3 (cf. 'ring')
wrinkle wrinkled: 4.1.1
write wrote writing written writer: 3.2.5 3.2.6 4.1.1 4.1.2 4.6.1 7.2.4
 7.3.5

Y
yield yielded yielding: 3.3.2
your (possessive)/you're (=you are): 3.2.5 3.2.6 7.3.5